Where we come from
2008

Where we come from 2008

✦

Piergiorgio Costa

iUniverse, Inc.
New York   Bloomington

Where we come from 2008

iUniverse books may be ordered through booksellers or by contacting:

iUniverse
1663 Liberty Drive
Bloomington, IN 47403
www.iuniverse.com
1-800-Authors (1-800-288-4677)

ISBN: 978-0-595-53158-5 (pbk)
ISBN: 978-0-595-63220-6 (ebk)

Printed in the United States of America

Table of Contents

The Costas

Eugenio 1861– mrrd. **Antonietta De Ferrari**
Children:
Giacomo 1896-mrrd. **Gina Parodi:**
Maria, Mario, Eugenio, Luigi, Antonietta, Enrico
Marianna 1899
Andrea 1901-mrrd. **Niccolina Musso**
Enrico 1903-mrrd. **Mimi Viganego**
Eugenio, Stefano, Nicola, Costanza

Enrico 1864-mrrd. **Victorine Dusson**

Federico 1866-mrrd. **Bice De Ferrari**
Children :
Pippo 1897-mrrd. **Angiolina Dufour**
Anna, Federico, Giovanna, Bice, Luisa, Giully
Caterina 1899-mrrd. **Antonio Cerruti**
Beatrice, Alessandro, Federico, Angelo, Filippo
Angelo 1901-mrrd. **Giuseppina Musso**
Giacomo, BB, Matia T, Nicolina, Maurizio, Cate, Franco, Paola, Enrica
Eugenio 1903-mrrd. **Maria Bozano**
Lorenzo, Bice, Pippo, Paolo, Carola, Antonio, Pio, Dome, Al, Michele, Sandro
Giacomo 1905-mrrd. **Anna Romanengo**
Maria, Piero, Angelo, Andrea, Bacci, Manuel, Gabry, Filippo, Josefa
Giovanni 1907- Jesuit
Federico 1914-mrrd. **Maria Pia Romanengo**
Franca, Giovanni, PG, Bernardetta, Beppe, Manuela, Federica, Michela

The Romanengos

Emanuele 1880 mrrd. **Rosetta Moro**
Children:
Tommaso 1907 mrrd. **Amalia Fera**
Emanuele, Stefano, Rusin, Andrea, Pai
Tonino 1908 mrrd. **Gigetta Rocca**
Paolo, Lorenzo, Mimma, Francesco
Teresa 1909 mrrd. **Alessio Dufour**
Puin, Bombi, Miccio, Giovanna, Pio, Armando, Mommi, Chicco
Maria 1911 mrrd. **Emilio Rota**
Maria Pia, Alberto, Carlo Emanuele, Maria Cristina, Maria Rosario
Maria Pia 1913 mrrd **Federico Costa**
Franca, Giovanni, PG, Bernardetta, Beppe, Emanuela, Federica, Michela
Francesca 1915
Mariangela 1919 mrrd. **Benedetto Santolini**
Malilla, Gabriella, Giovanna, Emanuela, Giovanni, Cedina, Federico, Francesca, Maria, Pio, Paola

Preface

I decided to write this book mostly because my daughters-in – law, Wendy and Christine, wanted to know more about our family and its roots. When I began, I was hesitant, and somewhat reluctant; I felt I lacked literary talent, and in addition, I saw the project as somewhat of an ego trip. As I continued writing, however, I began to enjoy myself. I discovered that I liked remembering past episodes in my life that I thought I had forgotten. I asked my sister Franca, and my cousin Giacomo, to help with my project and they gladly complied.

They both asked why I had decided to write this memoir, and supplied what they believed were my reasons for doing so. Franca suggested it could have been a form of therapy that would increase my self awareness, while Giacomo believed that by recounting our family history I was honoring my father's life. I don't think I did it for either reason, but I agree with Wendy and Christine that it is good for their children, my grandchildren, logistically separated from half of their family, to know more about their origin. This is not, however, my only reason. I have come to the conclusion that the ego trip theory may be my motivation after all. I would like my grandchildren to know how I feel about life, and what I believe is important. In the past I criticized my grandfather Federico's moral testament, and I want them to have the opportunity to do the same with my ideas and values.

I often feel that I have a problem expressing feelings and ideas, and by writing this memoir I hope that my grandchildren will come to know me. When it comes to remembering me, I don't want them to rely solely upon our occasional visits, and gifts that we have exchanged. This memoir is one a way to satisfy their possible curiosity; learning about the events of the past, and the way we were educated may help them better understand the Costa side of their family. (I do want to emphasize that in no way am I trying to impose my ideas on their education). At this point in my, life when more is behind me than in front of me, I am also doing my best to assess what I have accomplished. Franca may be right after all – this memoir may be an aid to self-awareness!

Whatever the reason behind my memoir, I hope it helps my readers appreciate our differences rather than fear them. We don't need to agree with each other on everything, but we should make an effort to understand all points of view. Good faith is no one's sole property.

I also want to say that while I might have made some errors in dates, or sequence of events, the facts are correct.

Regardless of that, I love you all.

1

Where We Come From: The Beginning

I was born on December 31, 1942, at noon, in Rapallo at 44 corso Colombo, which was just across the street from the small, local port. The first discussion my parents had about me was whether to register my birth on that day, or on the following day, January 1st, which would make a year younger.

Finally, they decided to follow what God or Nature had intended, especially when they recalled that a friend of my father's, also born on a December 31st had his birth registered on that date, and - years later - did not go to war because he was one year too old for it.

I've always been glad for my parents' decision, because I find that it is useless to try to cheat fate. What happens is what is meant to happen, one has to learn to deal with it.

Corso Colombo 44 – the number is 88 today –was the house that my grandfather built around 1905 for his family, it was next to the one owned by his brother, Eugenio.

After my grandfather's death in 1923, it was used as a summer house by my grandmother and her sons. In 1933, my uncle Pippo bought a villa on top of the hill that overlooked both grandfather's and Eugenio's homes. At the same time, the land separating the villa and the two houses below, were for sale, and the Costa brothers and cousins did not miss this opportunity to purchase this property on which they built five houses, and created a park to be shared by all. The old house was left to my father, and continued to be used by my grandmother.

When I was born it was usual for women to give birth at home. Hospitals were busy with the casualties of the war, and homes were believed to be far safer for mothers and babies.

I was named Piergiorgio Giacomo Maria. The Piergiorgio was for Piergiorgio Frassati, who was born at the beginning of the 20th Century, and who was renowned for helping the poor, and for his passion for social justice. (On a lighter note, he was also famous for hiking and exploring mountains). Not a bad guy to be named for.

Frassati died when he was in his twenties. He had contracted polio while helping the poor, and in those days, polio was often lethal. The Byzantine hierarchy of the Roman Catholic Church cited him only as Blessed – one rank below a Saint. This bothered me for years, but now that the Church has decided not to recognize St. George as a Saint, I've come to the conclusion that being acknowledged a Blessed is not too bad after all.

Following our family tradition, the name Giacomo honors my Godfather as well as a cousin, and Maria is to solicit the protection of the Virgin Mary. I was baptized in the Church of San Michele di Pagana, and my Godmother Anna once told me that it was a blustery, cold day, and I was garbed in many layers of beautiful, baptismal dresses which made me squirm, and she had a hard time holding me.

It was in that very same church where my wife, Silvia, and I were married in 1967, and where, years later, Alberto was baptized.

I was the third born child, and I had older and younger siblings, each separated from me by four- and-a -half years. In our family that was an oddity, because everyone else is just two years apart. I don't know if the war had something to do with this; a miscarriage might also have been the cause. Whatever the reason, I always felt that my mother had a special predilection for me. And I felt very close to her.

At this point I want to step back and try to explain the large branching out of our family. I will tell you about events, attitudes, and behaviors that today might make no sense to you. And I, who lived closer to those times, also have a hard time understanding everything that went on. I think that is a good thing. It means that customs and standards change and evolve, often for the better, and we should not be afraid of the new or the unknown.

My father's family were the Costas, and my mother's family were the Romanengos. Both families were part of the bourgeoisie which became prominent after the French Revolution and Napoleon. They believed in hard work, obedience to the law of the state, the social hierarchy, propriety, and the absolute right to own property. The men were the providers, the women ruled the home. They all abided by the authority of the Roman Catholic Church.

Obedience was a duty and a virtue. They were people of integrity, and their word was worth more than any signed contract. The world was clear to them: everything was either black or white, evil or good. Anything different was probably evil. Duty came before pleasure, and honor was important above all. They were slow on enthusiasm, but persevered for what they believed to be right. In a word - they were conservatives.

Both family were quintessential Genoese. Genoa and the region of Liguria, are squeezed between the Apennine mountains and the sea. It is a harshly beautiful land, with very little flat terrain available for building or farming. To gain space, the hillsides have been terraced in narrow flat tiers, with stone walls meant to hold the land back from sliding down. There are orchards and vineyards, and cultivating them calls for hard work, because machines can not be used on those narrow strips of land. A good part of Genoa is built on land regained from the sea. To survive, everyone must work, and nothing is wasted. This hard life explains the reputation the Genoese have for parsimony - it occasionally borders on stinginess - and also for a rustic, to-the -point character.

The Genoese also have a rebellious streak, having in past years fought against Milan, the French, and the Spanish for their independence. It was natural to look to the sea for expansion, and the Genoese became sailors and traders. Like all good traders, they are wary of the people they deal with. But, while a relationship starts slowly and moves with great deliberation, a friendship, once established, lasts a lifetime.

Genoa became an independent Republic in the eleventh century, and quickly expanded to encompass the entire Mediterranean, the Near East, and extended as far as the Black Sea, where the Genoese developed a profitable trade in spices and silks. The concept of a Republic then was not what it is today. The power was in the hands of a few rich families such as the Dorias, Spinolas, and Adornos . The citizens of Genoa, however, had rights that the Monarchies of the time did not grant. And having those rights inspired independent thinking on the part of the Genoese, and also an appreciation of private enterprise.

This free thinking was also extended, in part, to the contracts signed by the men who sailed from the port of Genoa. The sailors had a choice: if they negotiated for, and received, higher pay, they had no further rights. Complaints about working conditions or hard treatment were not permitted. However, if they accepted less money, they had the right to "mugugno", meaning the right to publicly express their grievances. It is said that the majority of Genoese sailors chose "mugugno". That is typical of the Genoese, who like to speak their minds to the point of being rude.

The Republic with its ups and downs prospered, and became an important banking center, loaning money to the Spanish, the French and the British crown. However, the discovery of America by a Genoese, at the service of a Spanish Queen, marked the beginning of Genoese decline. The local entrepreneurs, rich from past trading, did not recognize the opportunity, nor did they want to take the risk of the new challenge. They preferred to stay with old ways. A slow decline ensued, and by 1815 the region became a possession of the Savoia family.

I tell you all this because there is a clear correlation between the history of the city, and the history of the Costa company. At first, we took risks and grew. We worked hard. But then, after a time, we became complacent and lost our edge. There is a lot of the Genoese character in us, or at least in me.

Here are some curious facts about Genoa. The flag of the city, a red cross on a white field, was adopted by the English as their marine flag when the first British ship sailed to the Mediterranean under Genoese protection. It is still the flag flown by the British navy. The word "jean" comes from the name "Genoa" which was the appellation for the blue fabric sold in that city. On the other hand, Genoa salami is strictly a modern American creation. It is easy today to disagree with, or make fun of, the generations of years ago, but I respect their ideas and the way they lived.

2

The Romanengos

The Romanengos were confectioners who started their business in 1782. The Costas were traders in olive oil, and established themselves in 1854.

I don't know much about the Romanengos before my grandparents' generation.

I never met my grandfather, Emanuele Romanengo, who died of the Spanish flu right after World War I. The photo of him that I saw shows him with round spectacles, a full head of hair, and a stern look. My grandmother, Rosetta Moro, on the contrary, was a lot of fun to be around. Her family was fairly well to do, with a business in South America, and a huge villa on the outskirts of Genoa, complete with a stable and a tennis court. At that time, we were living in an apartment, and I was awed by the mansion. Since then, the villa and its surroundings have been converted into condominiums.

Nonna Rosetta was a very short woman, full of spunk, and always willing to close an eye to her grandkids' mischief. Her mother, Nonna Angiolina, was quite similar; she loved to have guests, and organized parties into her late years.

Nonna Rosetta was the first person I knew who bought a TV set. That was in the early fifties, and the TV was an additional reason to go visiting. Thursday was the best time, because "Lascia o Raddoppia", which means "Quit or Double", the first game show in Italy – was on Thursday nights, and we, and the rest of the country, were crazy about it. Tabloids made a living gossiping about the contenders. We would all watch - adults and children. The children sat on the floor in two or three rows, and the adults perched on every available seat. Nonna Rosetta presided, and sat in the place of honor – right in the middle of the three generations. I was very proud to be considered old enough to be there.

Christmas and Easter lunches were the other big Romanengo reunions held at Nonna Rosetta's house. I have memories of indigestion as I ate raviolis, turkey, and the always present Romanengo pastries. After the war, food was a big deal, and those feasts were something to look forward to.

Rosetta and Emanuele had two boys and five girls. They all married, except for Zia Francesca. She had been a nurse during World War II, and lived with her mother and looked after her. She was the only one who smoked, but at the time no one minded.

I was particularly close to Alberto, a cousin, whose father was one of my heroes. Emilio Rota was descended from generations of Navy men, and he was an officer in the Royal Navy during the war. When the war ended, and Italy became a Republic, he refused to pledge loyalty to the new constitution because he did not want to renege on his pledge to the King. He gave up his career on a principle, while another of his cousins stayed in the service, and became one of the top admirals in Italy. In retrospect, I'm not sure that I still subscribe to that idealism, but I still admire Emilio Rota. After he left the Navy, he lived a sad life, working at a job he did not care for. He was happy only when he was building wooden models of the Italian and British fleet which had fought in the Mediterranean.

Alberto and I were allowed to play with the models, which we did with the utmost care, because we knew they were something very special. Emilio's wife, Maria, was a great reader, and we spent many rainy afternoon listening to adventure stories which took place in far away places, and were written by authors who had never left Europe. We did not know that at the time, and those books were our windows to the exotic.

As we grew older, Alberto and I were not as close as we had been as children. Alberto died in his twenties in a mountaineering accident. Emilio and Maria also had three daughters and another son, and all the children were named after members of the royal family. They still live in Genoa, with the exclusion of Maria Cristina, who married a Canadian and live in Vancouver.

My aunt, Teresa Dufour, was the carbon copy of her mother, Nonna Rosetta, in body and in character. Her husband, Alessio, owned a candy factory and loved to have guests. He had a very good relationship with the local Bishop, and because of that, Midnight Mass on Christmas Eve was celebrated at his house every year. I still have nightmarish memories of those nights, as I did my best to fight sleep, and prove that I was old enough to be invited. The Dufours were a family of eight as were we. Several of the Dufours died young, in their thirties and forties, all of heart- related ailments. They were all funny, like members of a fraternity. Miccio, his real name was Emanuele, could have been the inspiration for John Belushi's character Blutho, in the movie "Animal House", had Belushi known him. The boys liked to hunt, and one summer in Voltaggio I went hunting with them. That was when I shot my first and last bird, a small poor thing. I felt so badly that I never shot an animal again. That, however, did not stop me from eating what the hunters brought home. I guess I have a distorted mind.

My uncle Tonino, and his wife Gigetta, had two boys close to my age, Lorenzo and Paolo. Tonino purchased the second television set in the family. I was a classmate of Lorenzo's for many years, and while we were friends, we did not share the same interests in adventures and sports. As an adult, Tonino was put in charge of the Romanengo confection company. He was in a German concentration camp at the end of WWII, and he never quite recovered his health. He died fairly young, in his fifties. The older son, Paolo, took his place at the factory until just recently. The family was completed by a daughter, Mimma, and a much younger brother, Francesco.

After the war, his brother, my uncle Tommaso, was looking for work, and my father suggested that he become involved in the reconstruction of our factories, which had been destroyed during the war. Forming a partnership, they started a construction company that branched out into residential buildings, and they became very successful. Many years later, Tomasso's son, Emanuele, bought out our share of the company, and was a big shot in that field for a while. Later, however, he became financially overextended, and went bankrupt.

Tommaso was a hypochondriac, and it was funny to see his wife, Amalia, do her best to brush off his presumed heart attacks. Amalia was a beautiful woman of German ancestry, as cold as ice, and she became even tougher after the death of her two sons, one in infancy, and the other, Stefano, in a freak accident during his teens.

Amalia and Stefano were taking a short hike, and Stefano climbed up on a small boulder. When on top, the boulder rolled down, and Stefano fell beneath it. Amalia tried to free him, but the boulder was too heavy, and she could not do it. She had to leave him there and run to look for help. I imagine that those few kilometers were the hardest walk of her life. Life, at times, serves us drama that outdoes the wildest fiction. Two daughters, Rosetta and Pai, completed that family.

The most fun family on the Romanengo side were the Santolinis. Benedetto and Mariangela had ten kids, all hyperactive, funny, and full of enthusiasm. They had five girls before the first of three boys were born, and then had two more girls, for a total of ten children. The laundry was so large that they gave up trying to sort out the clothes. The clean garments went into various dresser drawers, and it was up to the kids to search out their own stuff.

The oldest boy, Giovanni, became a missionary priest and was killed in the Congo. He had an early disposition for mysticism. His mother caught him on the ledge of their sixth floor balcony ready to jump, so sure that angels would come and catch him before he hit the ground. The second son, Federico, is my Godson, and became an orthopedic surgeon like his father. My uncle Benedetto and his brother, were totally bald from their teen years on, because their mother, trying to stimulate hair growth, used a lotion that had the opposite effect, and burned the boys' scalps, leaving them hairless and scarred. Instead of feeling ashamed, the boys used their wigs to play Frisbee in school. Benedetto retained his love of life no matter what happened. He was involved in politics, and was elected to the city council as a member of the Christian Democratic Party. Mariangela, the youngest of my mother's sisters, was my source of information for the history of the Romanego family.

The Romanengo confection factory and stores are still in operation, and they use pretty much the same manufacturing and packaging techniques that have been employed for the last two-hundred and more years. The Romanengos are extremely selective in the choice of ingredients that go into their products, and as a consequence, the cost of their pastries is well above that of the competition. My cousins have considered the possibility of compromise, thus making their products more cost effective. They are, however, good Genoese, adverse to the new, and decided to keep the tradition unchanged. The consequence is that their clients, mostly local, know and appreciate the superiority of their products. The expansion of the market, however, is almost non-existent. Should you go into one of their stores, the way your purchase is packaged is a show in itself. The same old style: cardboard trays and heavy white and blue paper are precisely alternated, with two seals, and two different types of strings. It takes several minutes for the task to be completed. Some times when people are waiting to be served, you can see eyes rolling, and feet shuffling, but that does not speed up the process. The Romanengo brand is sterling, but that excellent reputation does not convert to good profits.

3

The Costas

The Costa family is a little more complex than the Romanengos, and I'll start from the moment the "Giacomo Costa fu Andrea" company was founded.

In 1854 two brothers, Giobatta and Giacomo, started a company for the purpose of trading olive oil. They bought from various countries on the Mediterranean, and resold the oil in Italy. In 1860, the company was left to Giacomo. He and his four sons, Luigi, Eugenio, Enrico and Federico, expanded the business, opening olive oil refining factories in Italy and Spain. They also manufactured the cans which contained the oil. The trade was extended to North America, and sold under the brand names "Olio Costa" and "Dante". In 1905, Dante was awarded the Gold Medal at the St. Louis World's Fair, and in 1915 won the Gold Medal in San Francisco.

In 1924, the brothers decided that it was time to branch out, and made shipping the oil part of the family business. A small tanker, the Ravenna, was purchased, but the ship-owning business did not start under good auspices. There was a delay in delivery of almost a month after the ship was purchased. In the meantime, the oil market collapsed, and the loss on the oil that was waiting to be transported was more than the cost of the ship. All this did not discourage the brothers, however, and they bought more ships in 1928 and still more in the thirties. By then, the ships were no longer used mainly for transporting olive oil, but served third parties.

At the beginning of WWII, the company owned eight ships. Only the smallest, the Langano, survived the war, all the others were sunk in various convoys.

After the war, with the help of the Marshall Plan for Reconstruction of Europe, new ships were purchased, and this time, in addition to cargo, passengers trade was started.

The plan was to transport emigrants to Argentina and Brazil on the southbound trip from Italy, and return with badly needed agricultural products, grains and meat, on the northbound leg. The first ship, the Anna C, was converted to three classes of passenger service, and also carried bulk/refrigerated cargo. The small First Class would compare unfavorably today to local ferries. The Second Class was very Spartan, to say the least, and the Third Class contained dormitories divided according to sex, with common bathrooms and showers. To me, as a child, the ship was the quintessence of elegance and glamour. Before the maiden voyage, the company decided to treat the employees to a one day cruise to nowhere. I was only five, and not considered old enough to go. I pleaded my case with so much intensity, that at the end, my father gave up, and I was part of the now famous "crociera dei gatti" which translates to "the barf cruise". The ship did not go too far from Genoa. I suppose to save fuel, and she barely made it to Portofino.

Food was a big attraction then, and we all crowded into the dining room while a slow long surf rocked the ship. Gradually the room emptied, and the decks became a refuge for most of us. I stretched out, periodically emptying my stomach even when there was nothing left to regurgitate. The sky was gloomy, and the crew unhappy, for they had to clean up the mess. In retrospect, the only positive thing I can say is that I was part of company history.

In 1959, the company recognized that emigration traffic was slowing down and long distance passengers transportation was now airplane business. It was decided to try something luxurious and exclusive, something only the kings and aristocracy were known to enjoy: sea cruises. The Franca C, named after my oldest sister, was converted to a one-class ship, with facilities in all the cabins and one dining room. The ship was based part of the year in the Caribbean, and the remainder in the Mediterranean, offering seven and fourteen days cruises. It was an immediate success. It has to be noted that Grandma Puny was one of the first and best clients of the company.

After the war, seed oil factories were also added in the north and south of Italy, and new brand names, OIO and GICO, made of peanuts and soybeans respectively, were successfully marketed in Europe and Iran. A textile division was also started, creating cotton and silk fabrics for fashion designers.

The driving and glamorous part of the company, however, was the shipping, in particular the cruise business that was blossoming in the Mediterranean and most of all, in North and South America. Linea "C",as it was known at the time, was the first cruise line to sell packages that included air and cruise in one price, making vacation travel an easier sale for travel agents.

We'll return to the company history later on, when it will be a more important part of my life. Now I will go back to my Grandfather Federico and his brothers.

Like my grandfather from the Romanengo side, he died few years after the First World War. In his case, it was a heart attack, which my Grandmother Bice attributed to his passion for rowing. He was good at that sport, and was the Italian Champion of Solo Rowing for some years. Among the few pictures of him that I have seen, he is in his boat, wearing a silly striped bathing suit, which resembles boxers and a tank top. On his head he wore a little striped cap, similar to the one Babe Ruth wore. He also sported a square short beard like a goatee. He was a strict disciplinarian, a hard worker, and very religious. He left a moral legacy that was greatly esteemed by the family, but from which I dissented. He would say, "You have to be honest with your clients because it will benefit your business". I, on the contrary, believe that you have to be fair with your clients because it is the right thing to do. His idea was to give so that you will get more back. This is an approach to life that is classic, pragmatic, bourgeois philosophy. Not that it is untrue, or that it doesn't work, but I refuse to think of life as an accounting book. He also said that you had to respect your elders, and the authorities. In general, I have no problem with this statement. What he forgot to add, however, was that respect must be earned, and should not be offered blindly. Leaders should be held to the highest standard, and made accountable for their actions. No one should be obeyed blindly, or given undeserved trust.

Eugenio was my grandfather's oldest brother, and the closest to him. This was partially because he married my grandmother's sister, Antonietta. Eugenio owned the house next to my grandfather's house in Rapallo and I thought of his children as my uncles, and spent my summers with their kids who were living around us in Rapallo. I don't know much about him other than that he loved music, and had an easy way with people.

The only brother of my grandfather's whom I met was Barba Rico. "Barba" in Genoese dialect means uncle, and in Italian, means beard. Barba Rico sported a beautiful big white beard that made him look like Santa and therefore, the name was fitting. He was very jovial, and I loved it when he did his magic tricks, pulling candies for the children out of his beard. He loved to play cards, and my mother played with him. She was fond of Barba Rico, in part because they both had little love for my grandmother. My mother knew he won at cards because he cheated, but she never said a word to him about it. He also cheated while playing solitaire, and justified it, saying "it's just for fun".

When I grew older, I discovered another aspect of Barba Rico that made him more dear to me. He was a man full of life and lust, and the black sheep of the family. He was in charge of buying olive oil from the farmers in the south of Italy, and traveled around in a horse drawn cart. The farmers hid their daughters when they knew he was coming. His charm and good looks were irresistible, and many barns and haystacks saw his love activities. We probably have blood cousins down there that we haven't met.

As usual in life, he was paid back with the same currency. During one trip to Paris he fell in love with a Moulin Rouge dancer, Victorine Dusson, and took her back to Genoa, lavishing gifts on her. It was a big scandal in the fairly provincial local community. My Grandmother Bice somehow convinced him to save the appearance of morality, and he married the French woman who proceeded to run away with a new beau. I can't blame her, because she must have been treated icily and with contempt by the rest of the family, and Genoa must have looked very limited after Paris. Barba Rico lived with us during the war, somehow mitigating the discomfort of being under the same roof with a very stern Grandmother Bice. An additional benefit was that he was a good fisherman, and a friend of other fishermen. During those days when food was difficult to find, we never lacked fish, much to the displeasure of Giovanni, who hated it. He was forced to eat the fish by my grandmother, while my mother might have given him a break.

I remember my Grandmother Bice as very intimidating, with a mustache that scratched my cheeks every time I kissed her, not that many kisses were shared. I believe that her strict demeanor was more a façade than her real character. It was the result of an upbringing that, among other things, required her to address her parents in the third person, and allowed her to join them at the dinner table only when she was well in to her teens. They were not a warm and fuzzy group.

Grandmother Bice came from a noble family – not old nobility - new money as it would be called today. Her uncle, Gaetano DeFerrari, married Maria Annenkoff, the niece of the Russian Czar. Gaetano was a commoner, and he had to buy the title of Duke from the Pope, in order to gain permission for the marriage. He also bought the title of Marquis for his brother, Giuseppe, my great-grandfather, so that the whole family would be socially presentable. The wedding marked the last visit of the Russian fleet to Genoa until recent years. Gaetano had a reputation of being very stingy, like all Genoese. Every season, Maria went to Paris to buy the latest fashion, and he put her on a strict budget. If she came back with more trunks than expected, those trunks were locked in the attic as food for moths, and she was not allowed to wear her purchases. Stingy and stupid, if I may say so. She had the last word: she got him to restore a great villa on lake Garda where she built a famous garden that can be visited to this day. That made a dent in his assets. Gaetano and Maria's daughter married Prince Borghese, the grandfather of Marcella Borghese, who was founder of the Borghese line of cosmetics.

Back to my Grandmother Bice, she was never really part of her husband's life. Her involvement was limited to delivering seven children, and running the house.

Giuseppe, the oldest, was usually called Pippo. He was a short man, full of spunk, ultra-conservative, and bigoted. I can't help myself, but I liked him. He was the result of his time and education, and besides, I have a sweet spot for him, because he introduced me to golf.

He served in the front in the Dolomites during the First World War, and was in the midst of real battle. He had five girls and one boy, Federico, whom he treated like a child even when they worked together. As a consequence, Federico developed into a shy, and introverted person. Pippo's oldest daughter, Anna, was my Godmother, and she always spoiled me with the gifts that I really wanted, but my parents rarely bought for me. I remember with special fondness sets of little toy soldiers, complete with trenches and a fort. Zio (uncle) Pippo was in charge of the sales of our company's canned oil. He was short on patience with the marketing people and his credo was "The only important thing is to be paid". All other strategies were B.S. He believed in simplicity: go visit the client, make the sale, and collect the money. Anything else was a waste of time. The same disdain applied to all new techniques including music. He believed that after Brahms, music died, and he had a great passion for the classics. He made friendship with the great musicians of his time. Magaloff, Horowitz, Rubinstein, and Horzosky, among others, dined at his house, and his daughter, Bice, married Horzosky late in life and is now curator of his archives. When his youngest daughter, Giully, was courted by a young man of good family, but little means, he had him investigated by a private detective before agreeing to the wedding. It is ironic that this young man, Adriano, was able to create a very successful and profitable business, while other sons- in-law - who were accepted with open arms - ended up bankrupt. Life is full of irony. Pippo was named our guardian after the death of our parents, and came for dinner every week. I then had the opportunity to get to know him, and found redeeming qualities in him. His wife, Angiolina, was a sweet little woman who adored her husband and he, in turn, adored her, but make no mistake, he was the boss. I don't remember ever hearing her disagree with him.

The most famous of my uncles was Angelo. He was an economist, and after the war was named President of the Italian Industrialists & Ship Owners Association. He served in this position for many years. He was famous for his battles with the Communist and Socialist Unions that were very powerful at the time. He was a free market advocate, and that put him at odds with the Fascists during the thirties. He was also very religious, like the rest of the family, and subscribed with obedience to all that was said by the Roman Catholic Church.

He was powerful and respected even by his opponents who admired his honesty. That makes the following alleged story even more surreal. He fell in love with a girl from Turin, Nicolina Musso. He went to her father to ask for her hand, and was told that Nicolina had an older, unmarried sister, Pinuccia, and if he wanted to, he could marry her, but under no circumstance could Nicolina become engaged before Pinuccia. He then married the older sister, and his cousin, Andrea, married his first love.

During World War II he helped save many Jews, and protected their property, but later, at the request of the Church, he smuggled Nazi criminals to South America on the Costa Line. The most famous of them was Martin Bormann. For me, it was disappointing to learn that obedience to the Church was for him, and the rest of the family, more important than justice. I understand that too many killings had already occurred, and it was time for reconciliation, but these men were evil, and helping them meant that their sins were condoned.

Angelo looked like Marlon Brando in "The Godfather", and like that godfather, he was the unofficial CEO of all family activities which led to a long period of profitable expansion. Like all his brothers, he had many children, one of whom, Giacomo III, was my Godfather, and we will talk about him in more detail later on. Another son, Franco, is one of my best friends. Franco's twin sister, Catte, married my cousin, Emanuele Romanengo, who eventually bankrupted the building company begun my father and his.

Marriages between the Costa, Romanego, and Dufour families were quite frequent in the small, insular Genoese society. Angelo's second son, Maurizio, became a Jesuit priest. There were five girls in addition to Catte, all of whom married, with the exception of Maria T, and you'll meet her further on.

Uncle Eugenio, the father of eleven kids, married a beautiful woman, Mariuccia, who was able to retain her beauty through all those pregnancies. The nickname for this family was "I Quarti" which was the name of the suburb where they lived. The family lived in a huge, beautiful villa, and Uncle Eugenio was in charge of olive and seed oil purchases, production, bulk sales, and all by products for the company.

Uncle Eugenio was my official boss when I began working for the company, even though his oldest son, Lorenzo, was actually in charge. Lorenzo and his brother, Pio, married two of my Romanengo-Dufour cousins. Paolo, the third son, became a Jesuit, but left the priesthood because he disagreed with Church policies.

Two daughters, Bice, who married a Dufours, and Carola, who married Cesare, a Count with more title than money. The six youngest were all boys, and still live in Genoa.

Uncle Giovanni became a Jesuit, and held various prestigious positions. He was based in Turin for a long time before he was sent to Madagascar as a missionary. According to my grandmother, he was a handful as a child. Giovanni was in trouble frequently because he liked to go dancing, an activity considered sinful and decadent. I guess that becoming a Jesuit proves that he had not been corrupted by that passion.

Uncle Giacomo II, also called the Saint, was in charge of the cargo ships of the Costa Line, but he was better known for his philanthropy and religiosity. Hordes of panhandlers took up positions outside our offices to await his arrival or departure. He believed that in a society, everyone had a special function - just as the parts of the body. Some were the brains, others were the hands, but all were meant to work for the common good. Were this theory universally accepted, social unrest and envy would not exist. I see this approach as quite elitist, because I'm sure that those destined to be the assholes would rather be the brains, and who is to decide where each of us belongs?

Giacomo married Anna, one of my mother's cousins, and they had eight children. The oldest and a younger daughter became nuns, and one of the boys, Angelo, became a priest. I will talk about two of the sons – Piero and Emanuele – later on, and there were three other boys: Andrea, Bacci and Fillipo.

Bacci is my age, and ever since he was a boy he had a passion for animals. I remember him returning from a hike, holding his socks in his hand which were filled with snakes, frogs, and other prey. Today, he is doing what he likes because he works for Genoa's Aquarium and Rome's Zoo.

Filippo lived in Argentina when army generals were the dictators of that country. It was during the time when people were arrested without due process of law, and later disappeared. Filippo had to be very careful, because his political beliefs made him a potential target. He eventually returned to Italy.

The only woman, Aunt Caterina, married Antonio Cerruti, a rich and handsome man, whose main interest was hunting – and not only for game. He was great fun to be with, but I don't think he made her very happy. They had four boys and a girl. Caterina's grandson, Tony, lives in New York, and works as a tour operator, which is similar to what I was doing.

All my other second cousins, whom I improperly called my uncles, and who were sons of my Granduncle Eugenio, also worked for the company.

The oldest, Giacomo I, was an artist. He played the piano and organ professionally, and conducted orchestras. He was also an excellent photographer, and his pictures are well regarded today. He married Gina, who came from a fine, local family, the Parodis. I don't ever remember seeing her smile. Giacomo was in charge of the company's oil export, and because no one can be good at everything, he didn't do much to improve matters in that department. Giacomo and Gina had six children, all artistic, and with easy dispositions. Luigi, who is thirteen years older that I am, is the one I am closest to. One of the sons is a Jesuit priest, and Enrico, the youngest, was a good friend of Grandmother Puny's. Enrico moved to Monte Carlo where he married a rich widow, but they later divorced.

Andrea, the second son, married Nicolina Musso, my Uncle Angelo's old love, and they were the only family without children . Andrea was very concerned about his health, and took great care of himself. It is ironic that Andrea was the first cousin to die of natural causes. This should make us wonder about just how much – or little –control we have over fate. Andrea was in charge of the textile group of the company which did not see much growth.

My favorite was Uncle Enrico. He was fun loving and had a beautiful wife, Mimmi. He loved music, but his talent was not equal to his brother Giacomo's. In truth, while he was a horrible violinist, his collection of violins was world class, with a Stradivarius and a Guarnieri among them. He was invited to many concerts where he allowed better musicians to use his violins, Every year he organized a ski race in Crans sur Sierre for family and friends, and that is one of the reasons we bought a house there. His children, Nico and Lilla, both my age, lived next to us in Rapallo, and we were best f riends. Eugenio, his oldest son, also became a Jesuit, bringing to seven the number of clergy in our family. Stefano, the second son, divided his time between Argentina and Pavia, a little town near Milan. Stefano never worked for the Costa Group. Enrico was another member of the family in charge of the Textile Division where he did not distinguish himself as an entrepreneur. His wife, Mimmi, had a reputation for weak health, and in the summer we were forbidden to play in the garden between one and three in the afternoon because she needed her nap. She is still alive and well surviving the rest of her generation.

Also part of this family was Marianna, who never married, and joined an order of laic nuns. We did not see much of Marianna because she was busy with her charities. What I know about her comes from Uncle Pippo, who must have been fond of her, because she was a tomboy when young, and defiant of proper behavior. The influence of the Catholic Church on our family was great, as is evident by the number of relatives who joined some religious order. Only Uncle Pippo's family and ours were not part of that group.

4

My Parents

My father, Federico, was the seventh and youngest of his family, and he was named after his father, who was also the seventh child. My sister, Federica, is also the seventh in our family. In the present and future generations I doubt that this tradition will continue, because the name Federico is now given to a first or second born child.

My father was good-looking, of medium height, and had wavy, black hair. He was a good student, smart, and had a passion for sports and exploring the mountainous countryside. He was not a very good tennis player, though that was his favorite game. He lacked the killer instinct necessary to win. He started his working career in the olive oil department of the family company, but then, when the war started, he was drafted into the army.

When the war ended, my father, with the Romanengo and the Moro families – related to us from my mother's side - started a construction company, the SCI, planning to rebuild the factories that had been destroyed by bombing. The company eventually evolved into a full scale construction company. My father did not stay there long, because the Costa Company bought two British ships, the "Southern Prince" and the "Ocean Virtue". My father was in charge of transforming the ships into modern passenger liners. In time, the ships became the "Anna C" and the "Andrea C". After that, my father was in charge of the passenger division, and he was responsible for that division's rapid growth. He enjoyed the respect and admiration of his competitors. He was not a warm fuzzy guy, nor could he be, considering his mother. My mother, however, was able to bring out his lighter side. He loved opera, and I remember reluctantly going with him to the derelict opera house in Genoa. I did not like opera then, but I have to admit that those seeds developed in me a love for opera and classical music later on.

Strangely, while his brothers and cousins were collecting the objects that reflected their various hobbies and interests, my father did not even have a decent gramophone, (stereo did not existed then), nor did he own many records. I don't know if this was because we were the poor side of the family, or that he just did not like to spend money on frivolities. He was a conservative, and could not have been otherwise considering his family. Church, family and the King were his allegiances, and he never questioned what was said by those institutions. He was more involved in our upbringing than his brothers were with their children. Maybe because he was younger, or maybe because my mother strongly believed that men should be more involved in family life. He was available for us on weekends for hiking, ski trips, and soccer games, and he spent his vacation with us, participating in our activities. When he had to work on Saturday afternoons he occasionally took me with him to his office, and even better, I went with him when he had to visit one of our ships. It wasn't that I was curious about his work, but I was very proud to be part of adult activities. He and my mother had a very close relationship, they were on the same level, which was far different from the way my uncles treated their wives. My parents made decisions together, and they did not necessarily agree on everything. This might sound normal today, but back then, the wedding vow solemnly stated that it was the wife's duty to obey her husband.

My mother was the fifth of seven children. She was short, with straight black hair. She loved hiking in the mountains and sports, and she was good at them, in spite of the fact that she did not have much time to play. I remember her winning a tennis tournament in Selva after two years of not touching a racket. With her sisters and friends, she founded the first Women's Field Hockey team in Italy, and became Italian Champion of that sport. It has to be said that the competition at the time was quite minimal.

My mother was an anglophile, and admired the British style of dress and behavior and speech. The understatement, "Mr. Livingstone I presume", was one example, as was the obedient heroism as mentioned in the poem, "The Charge of the Light Brigade" by Tennyson, and as written about in the stories of Rudyard Kipling. Along with that, was the belief that deeds counted more than words, and that one competed for the pleasure of playing the game, and not merely to win. And most important, was the idea that you must never, ever give up. I know that perseverance is an important virtue, but some times it might border on stubbornness. I see this trait in many of us, including me.

My mother was an early feminist. She did not subscribe to the idea that business matters were exclusively the domain of men. She drove a car while none of her sisters or sisters-in-law did. She read the sport papers when no one else in the family did. My male cousins were very happy about that, because they obtained the papers after she had finished reading them. She believed, as I said before, that parents should spend more time with their children, even though it was not customary at the time. She was interested in the arts and ancient history, and I owe my interest in those areas to her. She also had a distinct sense of social justice, and supported the rights of women and the poor. Like my father, she had great respect for the institutions he honored. However, she could see that they were not infallible.

She was involved in our schooling, and I had mixed feelings when she supervised my homework. I appreciated the help, but hated that she did not settle for anything less than a full effort. A slap on your head was the result of coasting, and Giovanni did get an extra share of dessert because his room was messy. We had a lot of help in the house, but we were responsible for keeping our stuff in order. It was considered a lack of respect for the personnel if we did not clean up after ourselves. I approve of that. This giving your best at everything you do clashes with the lazy side of my personality, but it is a great idea. I can not say I always follow it, but I try, as should everyone.

My grandmother Bice was not too fond of my mother. In fact, she was not very happy when my father announced his intention to marry her. One reason was that he was the last of her children living at home, and the wedding would have left her alone. The other reason was that my Mom was very different from her other daughters- in-law, and I guess, for my grandmother, being different lowered the standard.

We had good parents; I did not always follow all their teaching, because times and situations change, and I became more critical of the concept of authority. Obedience and respect have to be earned, they are not a right of those who are older or more powerful. Religion is not so much how and to whom you pray in church, but rather how you live your life when you are outside of church. Frugality is a virtue, but you can indulge yourself without being decadent. Sex can be discussed openly, not as a secret matter. Diversity should be enjoyed, and not regarded with fear. With the easy ways of communication today, there are no excuses for being unaware. However, the principles of family, hard work, integrity, love, perseverance, respect for those less fortunate, and accepting responsibility for one's actions, are the tenets on which I try to base my life, and those tenets came from my parents. The best thing they did was to give us responsibilities. They kept us on a loose leash, and they trusted us. We made mistakes and got punished, but not having been too sheltered helped us develop self - confidence and independence. God knows we badly needed those traits later in life. Of course, we had our bumps and bruises, but I think we grew stronger because of them. I admire today's parents and the way they dote on their children, and dedicate a great deal of their time to them. Sometimes, however, I wonder if too much protection is not counterproductive. If you are too sheltered as a child, you are not prepared to deal with the adversities that eventually you have to face in life. On the other hand, there is no such a thing as too much love. So keeping the right balance is a fine and difficult line to walk.

The Costa/ Romanengo / Moro families, like others, had summer homes on the Apennines near Genoa. The Costas were in Savignone, the Moros in Borgo, and the Romanengos in Voltaggio, all places that were only a few miles apart.

The villas had tennis and bocce courts, and the young people on vacation met for tournaments and socials. My parents met at one such tournament, and it was love at first sight. My aunt Mariangela told me that the night my mother met dad for the first time, she confided to her "I'm going to marry that guy", and she did. I gather from this, that she was as determined as he was.

My parents married in Genoa on the 25th of May, 1935; the reception was held at Grandma Rosetta's house. At the time, it was considered extravagant to rent an outside place for a reception. My father was twenty-four, and my mother was twenty, not an unusual age for marriage at that time. March of the following year my sister Franca was born, followed in July, 1938, two years later by my brother Giovanni.

5

Fascism and War

At first, my family did not join the Fascist party, they were solidly for the monarchy. Like the majority of the country, though, they were forced to join the Fascist party in 1934, because a law required membership in the party in order to be in business. When the King named Mussolini head of state, they accepted his decision without any dissent. This acceptance was reinforced when Mussolini made peace with the Vatican. The Church was at odds with the monarchy, because territories that the Pope had governed before Italy was united into one country were lost to him. The Lateran Pact brought most of the Roman Catholic Church clergy to the Fascist side. Many saw the Fascists as the best defense against communism and atheism, and besides, the Church has a history of siding with the powerful.

Fascism came to power because, after the First World War, Italy went through a period of unrest. The fear of a repeat of the Russian Revolution was in the minds of people who had something to lose. The government was not in control of finances, nor of public order. Fascists presented themselves as the party of order, responsibility, and patriotic pride. Patriotism was a big part of the message. I think it is right to love your country, but too many times in history this love has been manipulated for the benefit of the ones in power. If you are not with them, you don't love your country, shame on you! Also, our family answered the patriotic call, and when the government asked, our parents donated their gold wedding rings to support the war effort. But then again, you did not question the authorities, you obeyed.

Fascism got its name from the Fasciae, the symbol of the Roman legion. The Fasciae was a bunch of sticks tied together with an axe in the middle. The meaning is evident, each stick is breakable by itself, but held together with the rest, is very strong. The axe represents the force of the leader. All that played well to the middle and upper classes. The suppression of the opposition was deemed a necessary evil to bring the country back to normality. How many times in history have we seen this happen! You trade freedom for safety. In the short term it might work, but in the long term you'll regret it.

We owned factories in Spain at the time that the Civil War was raging, with atrocities perpetrated by both sides. Italy had "volunteers" fighting for Franco, but many Italians also fought in the International Brigade, on the Republican side. I suspect that the sympathies of our family were for Franco, because he officially defended the monarchy and the Church. Not to mention that we had property at stake.

In 1940, Italy declared war on France, Greece and England, and my father was drafted into the army. He was never sent to the front because he had children, and probably, because of friends that he had. He was stationed instead in Genoa.

In 1940, the Allies bombed the city from the sea and from the air, because it was an important port, and had shipbuilding industries. It became more and more dangerous to live in town. After one more bombing, our parents decided, along with our uncles and cousins, to move the family and part of the offices to Rapallo. It was a good decision, because the house where we had lived was totally destroyed, and more than nine-thousand civilians died in the city and region due to the bombing.

My sister Franca has a vivid memory of that move. My Grandmother Bice was already in Rapallo when our family, accompanied by our Dufour cousins, arrived at night, tired after an adventurous trip. At the top of the stairs of the villa, waiting for them, stood Grandma, threatening punishment to those who did not behave. Quite a warm welcome! Franca was reminded of Snow White's evil stepmother, the Dark Queen. She had seen that Walt Disney movie the year before, and still was terrified of the Queen.

Rapallo was also bombed by the Allies; the small port and the railway were considered strategic targets. The scale and number of the attacks were much smaller than in Genoa. Not so for Recco and Zoagli, two villages nearby, that had the misfortune to have railway bridges. Those town centers were totally leveled, while the bridges sustained only minor damages. I remembered those ruins for quite a few years after the war. The amount of bombing was enough for our uncles to decide to move inland, away from the port, and Grandma went with them, and I'm sure we did not miss her. My parents decided to stay, even though we were close to the port, probably because my mother did not want to leave her sister Teresa's family in Rapallo, and also it would have been too difficult for my father to commute from Genoa to visit us.

In the basement of our house a bomb shelter was created by reinforcing the ceiling with wooden beams. It was a room about four by fourteen feet, and I swear I remember being there. The last attack happened when I was three years old at most, so my memories might come from the stories I heard later on. I have, however, a vivid memory of a platform at the far end of the room, with a mattress, on which Franca and Giovanni slept, and a memory, too, of my wicker crib and another mattress for the adults. Fortunately, the house did not suffer a direct hit, because I'm not sure how safe that shelter was. In the garden, one morning, after a bombing, we found a large piece of train track from the railway that was hit one mile away. We saved that and it is probably still in the basement. Across the street from the house there was a sea wall, to protect against the enemy's landing. One night in 1944, the Germans executed six captured partisans, putting them up against the wall and shooting them. That portion of the wall, with bullets marks, was saved after the war as a memory of that barbarity.

It is necessary now to summarize the historical events of the times. This will help you better understand the decisions and behaviors of the people involved.

As said before, in 1940, Mussolini, who had a close relationship with Hitler, decided to join Germany's war effort. It has to be remembered that the Germans were then winning big time, and, probably, Mussolini assumed it would be an easy and short war. Italians like winners, and they are not the only ones who like them. But in Greece and Africa the war did not proceed easily, and the help of the German troops was needed. As a nation, we have never excelled at war, and the army was commanded mostly by incompetent generals who owed their positions more to their loyalty to the Fascist party, than their professional ability.

In the summer of 1943, the allied troops landed in Sicily, in spite of Mussolini's bombastic promise that the sacred land of the nation would never be occupied by its enemies. As I said, Italians like winners, and the Fascists were now on the loosing side. A group in the government loyal to the King deposed Mussolini, and had him arrested. The King named the old general, Badoglio, as head of the government, with the secret mandate to negotiate a separate peace with the Allies. On September 8, 1943, an armistice was announced on the radio. The King and government were safely relocated to American occupied territory. What followed was one of the darkest pages in Italian history.

The army received no instruction as to what it should do, it knew only that the hostilities with the Allies were over. The Germans now considered the Italians as their enemies, and they did not waste any time in surrounding and making prisoners of the Italian soldiers they found in their barracks; they sent them to prison camps in Germany. Some units, with brave commanding officers, resisted the Germans and were massacred. Other soldiers were able to put on civilian clothes before the Germans arrived, and they went home, or joined the partisans. In the meantime, the Germans freed Mussolini, and he organized a new republican government in opposition to the King. Civil war ensued between the Italians who were either on the left, or for the King against the Fascists and Mussolini.

The soldiers who made it home were in danger of deportation, or worse, unless they joined the new Fascist army. Some hid, some joined the army, others went to the mountains and became partisans.

On September 8th, my father was in an army base in Genoa. He decided to leave the base, and went to Rapallo, were he hid in the basement of my Uncle Pippo's house. It was a good decision to leave, because the soldiers who stayed were either killed, or deported to concentration camps in Germany.

I would have preferred my father to have joined the resistance, but I understand the reason why - many like him, and they were the majority - did not.

They were not egoists or cowards, but they saw in the partisan antifascist group parties and individuals of the left, whom they had despised before the Fascists took power, and they were unwilling to join them. They took an additional risk in not joining Mussolini's new army either, but they did not want to side with him and the Germans.

After the Second World War, there was a referendum to decide if Italy still wanted a King and the Savoia family, or if the country should become a republic. My whole family voted for the monarchy and lost.

It was in the midst of all these historical events that my life began.

6

How We Lived

We were born with so-called silver spoons in our mouths, but my parents made sure we were never aware of it. All indulgence had to be earned, and any non- essentials were a waste, and waste was the worst sin. My parents believed in tough love, physical punishment was used not to hurt you, but to make a point that bad behavior had consequences. Franca reminded me of a story buried in my memories. I was a bed wetter when three or four, and my mother threatened to burn my behind if I did not learn to stay dry. One day, after another wet night, she lit a newspaper and laid me on the kitchen table saying that this time she had had enough. Of course, nothing happened, and I'm not even sure that it was my last time of peeing in bed, so I reserve judgment as to the validity of the system. My Dad used to pinch our arms or pull our ears rather than spanking us - which was my Mom's approach. These physical punishments were normal in those days, and compared to other children we had it easy. Rarely I remember my Dad losing his temper with us. Occasionally, however, he went into great rages, and you did not want to be around him then. Screaming and yelling was the usual way of communication in many of the other Costa families. I'm not sure if we had some anger management issue in our genes, or if it was the norm at the time.

My memories of the war are minimal, and I rely on stories I heard afterwards. I do remember, however, when the British troops arrived in Rapallo, and occupied my uncle Enrico's house, which was next to ours. The house became the headquarters of an English Major, and for the first time in my short life I was exposed to unlimited sweets – tins of them. During the war, sugar was rationed, and impossible to find. Tins of concentrated milk became my favorite, and because I was a toddler I was always successful in begging for them. I don't remember being embarrassed by that, though I should have been. Food in general was scarce, meat in particular, and the tins of Spam,(the canned meat, not the junk mail), was a coveted item.

During the war we lost all our cars. Actually, it is more accurate to say they were requisitioned by the Germans after the 8th of September armistice. Mom was very sad to have lost her beloved Topolino - the small car she had been driving. The car was hidden with others behind a fake wall in a public garage to save it, but someone ratted, and the Germans arrived, knocked down the wall, and took the cars. After the war Dad bought her a new Topolino, this time the station wagon model. To be clear, even in that version, the car was no bigger than today's Mini Morris.

Another source of memories is a diary that my uncle Pippo kept during the years 1944/45. From that diary, I learned how everyone struggled with the food shortage, and with the fear of daily bombing, thanking God to escape it - even though others might have been hit. The requisition of all vehicles, including bicycles and other valuables, was also feared. Precious things were hidden, and many were damaged by mildew and humidity. I also learned that my Mom saved some of my uncles from been taken hostages by the Fascist militia. She would run on ahead of them, warning my uncles that the militia was on its way. And my one uncle who was taken was released, unharmed.

In 1946, with the war over, we moved back to Genoa to an apartment we rented because our old house had been destroyed during an air raid. It was a dark place, with only two bedrooms, and my crib was placed in the dining room. Because of the lack of space, Franca boarded at school during the week, coming home only on weekends. The arrangement made her sad, she hated being away from the rest of us. The most vivid memory I have of the apartment is chasing up and down the stairs after a huge rat, with my brother Giovanni, while the doormen swung at it with their brooms.

Fortunately, we did not stay in that apartment for long, and moved down the street to the top floor of an old villa. The villa belonged to the Marquis Borzino, and the last floor, the servants' quarters, had been damaged by bombing. My father made an agreement to reconstruct that floor in exchange for a long lease.

That was the house of my dreams. It had a small garden, but we had free access to the larger one of the Marquis. There I learned a tough lesson. The Marquis had a beehive, and Giovanni decided that it would be fun to stir up the bees. He took his sling and few pellets, and went on a hunting trip. I, who never to refused an adventure, tagged along. The bees did not appreciate our bombing and swarmed in our direction. We ran away as fast as possible with Giovanni rotating his sling over his head in an attempt to chase away the assailants. I was slower, and without a sling. The end result was very painful, with arms, face and legs swollen for days.

The house was a 17ᵗʰ century villa, full of nooks, and with rooms in all different shapes. Our floor was not on one level, and there was at least one step between rooms. From the large balcony you could access the slate roof, and I loved to climb up there and spend hours looking at the view, with my adrenalin pumping, because I knew I doing something forbidden and dangerous. Like Rapallo, we had many bedrooms, but few baths. The bedrooms, however, had sinks, so that we could wash our faces and teeth in them. A bath was a weekly event, and showers hardly existed in those old villas. None of that bothered me. I guess the stereotype of Italians not being clean has some basis. (To put your mind at ease, I want to state that we changed our habits on this matter).

We spent eight or nine happy years in that villa, and all my new brothers and sisters, with the exception of Michela, were born there.

In July of 1947 we went to the mountains on vacation. My Father drove us there, and left us under the surveillance of my aunt Mariangela. Our Mother was not there. That was quite unusual, and I could not figure out why. The strongest memory of that vacation is that Franca and Giovanni liked to put salt on their hands, and let the cows and the goats lick them. That seemed very daring and dangerous to me, and I wanted to do the same. I put salt on my hand, but as soon as an animal got close, I couldn't stop myself, and I pulled my hand away. I was not as brave as I thought. Finally, after few days of this, Zio Benedetto, who was not yet married to Zia Mariangela, took my wrist, and held it until my hand was wetly cleaned by a goat. After that, seeing that I still had my hand, I became courageous, and showed off to anyone who cared to watch. Sometimes I'm puzzled by modern child psychologists who oppose such forcing. As far as I'm concerned, it worked,and I was able to control my fears.

One day my Father came back, and the mystery of my Mother's absence was revealed. Bernardetta, our younger sister, had just been delivered. Even though I was almost five, no one explained to me how babies came into the world, and I still believed that the stork brought them. That, and the mystery of Santa, was explained to me in first grade by a better informed classmate. What a bad system! I felt inadequate, and somehow betrayed, when I learned the truth.

To me, Bernardetta was the most beautiful baby in the world. She had round full cheeks, and black eyes. I'm not sure if I started her nickname of "bimba bella", (beautiful girl), but for a while, that is what I called her. That early admiration did not stop me from taking advantage of her later on. The story goes like this. She was eleven or twelve, and afraid to sleep by herself.

My room was across the hall from hers, and she asked if I would sleep with the door of my room open. It's no excuse that I wanted to keep my door closed, and I'm ashamed to say that I asked for part of her weekly allowance in return, and she reluctantly paid me. To this day she does not miss an opportunity to remind me of my Scrooge-like behavior, and she's right.

In the fall after her birth, I started school at the private kindergarten of Signorina Ricchini. She was an old maid in my eyes, and she was probably in her thirties. My whole family started school with her. My first day there was miserable. I cried from the moment my mother left me, until she came to pick me up at lunchtime. I sat in the entrance by myself, hoping to create some sympathy for my despair, without any success. The next day, considering that I could do nothing to avoid being there, I decided that I might as well enjoy it, and it soon became fun.

The school was a little more than one kilometer from home, and after a few days I was allowed to walk there on my own. Traffic was minimal, and I guess the world was a safer place then. Whatever the reasons, to be given that responsibility helped me gain independence and self-esteem. I did not attend school a lot that year. I went through all the possible childhood illnesses, some of them, like diphtheria, twice, though I do I think that it is a scientific impossibility. Our pediatrician, Dr.Cattanei, prided himself on being a great diagnostician, but he really preferred social chit-chat to practicing medicine when he made a house call.

During the summer, we attended what, for many years, was the center of Rapallo's vacation activities: I bagni Molo. That was a sort of beach club, where we, and all our cousins, rented cabins for the season. These clubs had existed before the war, but were closed during the hostilities. The club was located on cement blocks that protected the port from the outside sea, and it had a small pebble beach, and concrete platforms with lounge chairs. Our beach season started at the beginning of June, and finished at the end of September. In August we took a break, and went to the mountains.

We usually walked to the club at nine in the morning, and returned home for lunch and a hated siesta. Most days, we returned to the club late in the afternoon. My aunts believed that at least two hours had to pass after a meal before going swimming. The cold water would halt digestion, they said, and death could result. Our family did not adhere to that theory, and I'm glad to say we all survived.

I learned to swim that summer, not that I wanted to, because I was very happy with my cork lifesaver. One afternoon I was nagging my older cousin Luigi, and to make me stop, he picked me up and threw me into the deep water. I made it back to the platform, spitting salt water, and the lifesaver was not needed again. Just like that time with the goats and cows, a little forceful approach obtained results - in spite of what a modern child psychologist might recommend.

We had a little dinghy, the "Pimpi", that I loved to row. The big boat was the "Il Cigno", the swan, and it measured ten feet, and had an inside motor that was constantly in trouble. You knew what time you were leaving, but when you would return was a question. The official owner of the Cigno, was my uncle Andrea, but the authorized users were Luigi and his brothers. With that boat it was possible to go much further than with the dinghy, but as one of the little ones, I was rarely allowed on it. My complaints about this huge injustice is what got me tossed into the water. Our bathing suits were made of wool, and with frequent contact with the sea water were itchy and rough by the end of the season.

The king of the fishermen was Giovanni, which is ironic, because he hated fish, and never ate what he caught. One of his heroic deeds was using his bare hands to capture a large octopus, and the tentacle marks on his arm lasted the whole summer, and were shown with pride, and envied by me.

Our villa in Rapallo had ten bedrooms, three toilets, and one bathroom !! When it was built, one bath per week was considered enough to keep everyone clean, and that standard did not change much by the time I grew up. To be naked in a bath tub had some connotation of sin, and some priests suggested bathing with underwear on. In Rapallo there was no need of bathing, because we spent the day in the water anyway !! Every year in Rapallo I had to endure what for me was a scary experience: the feast of Monte Allegro's Madonna. The main celebration included three days of huge and loud fireworks. The last two nights the event was held at midnight, and I was considered too young to stay up that late. That did not make much sense. You could not possibly sleep with all that noise just outside our garden. The fact of not seeing lights, but hearing the bangs. was very scary to me, and I remember holding my breath in terror waiting for the next noise. The fear disappeared when finally I was allowed to stay up and watch.

During the month of August, for my father's vacation, we went to the mountains. For a few years, we rented houses, but after a vacation in Val Gardena in the Dolomites, Dad decided to build a house there, in Selva.

At that time Selva was spectacular, still very undeveloped, rocky mountains so close you could touch them. In the summer we went hiking, mushroom hunting, bathed in frigid Alpine lakes, played tennis, and did rock climbing. Here, again, Giovanni excelled. With the help of a local guide he climbed many difficult rock faces, some of them never climbed before. I was limited to easier climbs which I enjoyed, in spite of feeling some vertigo. In Selva, we made many friendships with other vacationers from Milan, Turin, and Rome, as well as with local residents. That was an eye opener, because with very few exceptions, we knew only relatives and other Genoese. We were brought up with the feeling that strangers were to be looked at with suspicion, and that our ways were the only right ones.

Our closest friends in Selva were the Rivas, a family from the Veneto region, with eight children, just like us. They also built a house in Selva, and twice a year we skied or played together. Giovanni was briefly engaged to Piera, one of the Riva sisters. My friends were Felice and Costanzo, both about my age and both excellent skiers.

Christmas vacations were the other times we went to Selva. We would leave the night of the 25th by train, arriving the next morning without much sleep. The train station was located in the bottom of the valley, and from there a smaller train or a taxi would take us to our house. Without wasting time, we were off to the slopes in the usually frigid temperatures. Selva, at Christmas, was so cold that we'd ride the chairs wrapped in blankets.

Skiing equipment then was awkward, and hard to put on. Getting dressed in the morning was also torture, and as much as I liked Selva, I hated those vacations. I made myself a promise that as soon I had a say in matters I would only ski in February or March, when the weather was warmer. We didn't have vacation time during those months, so from the ages of fourteen to eighteen I quit skiing - with the exception of weekend trips to mountains near Genoa.

Rapallo and Selva were two of our places to vacation, along with short visits to Voltaggio in the Apennine hills near Genoa, where we spent a few days with the Romanengo side of the family.

In November of 1948 another brother, Beppe, was added to our family, followed at two years intervals by three sisters: Emanuela, Federica and Michela.

In the mean time I began first grade at the "Istituto Arecco", a Jesuit school that was attended by boys of the good local families. The girls attended two schools: "L'Assunsion" and the "Marcelline", both managed by nuns. My sisters were "Marcelline" girls.

Franca was a very good student, while Giovanni was always in trouble. I was pretty good, but had a hard time with penmanship and reading out loud. I remember cramped fingers, while Mom made me write my homework over and over again.

The "Arecco" was a large school, and it went from first grade to high school. Beside academics, they had lot of sports, both intramural and also outside of the school. That was unusual, because the public schools did not offer sports . Our classes were held every morning, including Saturdays, from 8.30 to 12.30, and every afternoon from 2.30 to 4.30. The only afternoons off were on Wednesday and Saturday, when intramural games were held. We would go home for lunch, so we walked the approximate mile that separated home from school four times a day. In our family we adopted Bill Cosby's joke, claiming that when I was a child, I had walked four miles barefooted, up hill both way and in the snow when I went to school. This was said every time I criticized my children for driving, or being driven to school.

My dream was to be a great soccer player, but really, I was quite bad. My redeeming grace was my enthusiasm, and my constant practicing, which made me barely passable. In absence of talent, practice and enthusiasm can make you decent at whatever you want to do, so that nothing is out of your reach. I also loved basketball, but with my height, I had little possibility of succeeding. I mostly warmed the bench of the varsity team, but I was allowed to play some minutes. Never when the game was on the line, though.

My Mother did not like make-up, or dressing a la mode. When there were Parents' Days at school, I remember being embarrassed by her plainness. I wondered why she could not be like Mrs. Demchenko, the mother of Alex, the most popular kid in the grade. He was of Russian origin, good at everything, and always ready with a quick and sassy answer to the teacher. Mrs. Demchenko was always perfectly made-up, with red lipstick and nails. I wish I could say that in the end she was a bad mother, just to make the point that appearance means nothing. The fact is that I don't know. She, however, represented what our culture told me to mistrust.

This is probably one of the main complaints I have about our education.

We were taught that everything that was flashy and ostentatious had to be a fake, and anything different should not be trusted. If someone was a witty conversationalist he was probably lying. Action was more important than words, and there was no need to experiment with, or try, new methods or ideas. While there might be some truth in this philosophy, refusing the unknown without examination is a crippling approach to life. I'm not advocating crazy adventures, but if you are given a chance to try something new, I think you should take it. I feel embarrassed that once I suggested prudence to someone, giving as my reason that for every Christopher Columbus who discovered America, there are many explorers who died trying. We would probably still be in Italy had I not eventually grown away from these teachings.

At six I was old enough to be teased by my older brother Giovanni, and he did not miss an opportunity to do so. I was too small to defend myself by fighting, and therefore I cried. Tears were my way of protesting the injustice that I felt he was submitting me to. Tears, however, created the opposite effect, instead of attracting sympathy they brought on more teasing. I was nicknamed crocodile; I still don't know why crocodiles are supposed to cry, but every time my eyes started to water Franca and Giovanni intoned a chant, " crocodile, crocodile". My parents did not intervene, I assume because they wanted me to show more fortitude. Finally, their strategy worked, and my crying fits disappeared. My sister Manuela did not go through that sort of harassment, and kept on crying well into high school.

7

Growing up

My elementary school days were uneventful, I got good grades, and worked hard on my reading and penmanship. Signorina Guiglia was my teacher for all five years of elementary school. She was a short woman, and had been a nurse with my aunt, Francesca Romanengo, during the war. She liked me, or so I thought. She found my confusing letters - such as Gevona instead of Genova – funny, even though today it's recognized as a sign of dyslexia, a condition totally unknown at the time. She also found my lisp charming, (the word is "pesseta" in Genoese), and she would ask me questions that required an answer with the letter "s" because she thought it amusing. I was not offended, I thought I was a funny guy.

I hated reading, until the day I was given a little book of adventures that I could read on my own. That event was a revelation, I could read, and it was fun. I would read at night, way past my bedtime, with a lamp under the covers, so as not to be discovered. Television became the worst enemy of reading later on. My other great discovery were the movies. There was a movie theatre next to our house run by the Franciscan Friars. If there was no soccer Saturday or Sunday afternoon, there were the movies, and I would be in the theatre from the first show until dinnertime. In Italy then, you could sit in the theater as long as you wanted, so I watched the same movie two or three time in a row. Because of the proximity to home I was allowed to go alone, and right there I discovered America. Most of the movies were Westerns or war movies. John Wayne, Richard Widmark, Errol Flynn etc., were either marines, sheriffs or in the cavalry. John Ford introduced me to Monument Valley, and others western locations. Apaches and Sioux were the bad guys, while the blue bellies always saved the day, and the Marines' "Battle Hymn" was my favorite song. I would have loved to wear army fatigues, or blue pants with a yellow stripe and a cowboy hat, but even if they were available my mother would never allowed them; that would have been a waste of money and a concession to appearance.

Another Sunday activity during the winter was to go to the stadium and watch Genoa's soccer games. In the family, we were all for the Genoa team, except for Giovanni, who was for Sampdoria, the other local team. One of the few times that I saw my dad lose his cool was during the games, when the referee made a bad call. Genoa's was a lousy team with a great tradition, and it is still that to this day. All Genoa team supporters are irrationally passionate, but rarely get respect or satisfaction. The good teams were from Milan and Turin, somehow reflecting the economic fortunes of those cities. That situation fed our underdog mentality - us against the rest of the world – and it's a mentality that I still have.

At home, the family had at least four women in help. A cook, two maids, and a nanny. Still, meat was not eaten every day because it was too expensive, and desserts were rare. The household help was part of the family, and stayed in service for long periods of time, with a little bit of plantation mentality. It was, looking at it today, a weird arrangement, but the lady of the house was not supposed to do any household chores, and I don't remember my mother ever cooking, or my father changing a diaper . Thursday afternoons and Sundays were the days off for the help. In our family, Thursday night was when we ate our favorite dinner - a sort of big brunch - with toast, ham, focaccia, assorted cheeses, and cakes that could be prepared in advance. It definitely beat the greasy stews, tripe or liver that were on the menu many other nights. Also working for us from time-to- time, was a Swiss au pair, who was supposed to teach us French, then considered more important than English. All in all, I'm happier with today's less formal life style, and the fact that parents are more involved with their kids.

Middle school started when I was eleven, and still wearing short pants. My legs were bowed, and at that age, started to develop black hairs, which embarrassed me greatly. I pleaded with my mother, and she finally bought me long pants. With only one pair, I was determined to wear them every day, and learned to put the pants under the mattress at night to hold the crease. It was for me, a big deal to be one of the few boys not wearing that adult symbol. My self- esteem depended on that simple piece of clothing, and I guess that is very Italian: looks are everything. My mother eventually took pity on me, and bought me another pair, and my honor was saved.

My teacher for Italian, Latin and History was a Jesuit, Fr. Casassa. He was very good, and made learning fun. I still remember him dividing the class into two groups, the Greeks and the Trojans, when we were studying the Iliad. Each of us portrayed a character in the story, and each team would get points according to our grades. My grades were good, and so was life.

During the summer of seventh grade, I was sent to Switzerland, to an all female boarding school near Geneva to improve my French. At first, I was not very happy, expecting to be bored. But I discovered that girls were not bad after all, and had a great time. Nothing salacious, but friendships with people from different cultures and background. There, for the first time in my life, I met children of divorced parents, as well as girls who grew up in Africa, some of whom were Moslem. I realized that these young people were quite like me. It was an eye- opening experience. The nuns who ran the school told my parents when they came for me, that I would be too old to attend their school the following summer.

8

The Accident

They say there is quiet before the storm, and I agree. I get nervous today when all goes too well, because I expect life to blindside me when I least expect it.

Our family had just moved into a new house, a duplex with a large balcony, and more rooms. It was built to our specifications, and was very nice, even though I missed the old villa. Our youngest sister Michela was born, Franca had graduated from high school and was getting ready for college, and I had graduated from middle school, and was looking forward to the emancipation of high school.

It was the summer of 1956, we had just bought a new car, a FIAT 600, a small utility vehicle that replaced the beloved Topolino station wagon, our second car. Franca had just left for the USA, where she was sent to learn English as a guest of a New Hampshire family. Giovanni, as usual, was taking summer remedial courses in order to be allowed to move up to the next grade.

My Dad had to attend a shipping conference in Paris, and my Mom saw it as a great opportunity for a trip to France. I was the oldest available child, and excited to be the one chosen to go with them. The new car needed some miles to break it in, so the older and larger and stronger 1400 was left home, and off we went.

It was my first real trip abroad, the Swiss boarding school did not qualify as a trip, and I loved every minute of it. First it was the Cote d'Azur, then Provence, including Arles and Aix. I wanted to see a bullfight in Aix, but my Mom was opposed, saying it was a barbaric show. We then visited some of the chateaux in the Loire Valley, and I was awed by their beauty and sense of history. I also enjoyed the different food that the region offered. We stopped briefly in Chartres to see the Cathedral, and then went on to Paris. New wonderments at the Louvre Museum, where I saw the Mona Lisa, and The Winged Victory of Samothrace.

The only bad new was the sinking of the Andrea Doria, the flag ship of the Italian fleet, in a collision with a Swedish ship, the Stockholm, near Nantucket. To be truthful, I did not care all that much, because I was in heaven with lots of things to absorb. After three days in Paris we started back, on our way home, going this time through the region of the French Alps. We stopped for the night in Briancon, just before the Monginevro Pass, the same one used by Hannibal to invade Italy almost two-thousand years before.

The next day we left early, intending to be back in Rapallo for lunch.

I could not wait to get there, and to go to the beach and to brag to my friends and cousins about all the wonders I had seen.

It was July 30th, my mother was driving, and I was sitting in the back, sharing the seat with a suitcase that did not fit in the small trunk of the car. We had crossed the border easily, and reached the flat valley where we hit traffic. We were proceeding in a line at a moderate speed, and so were the cars coming from the opposite direction. All I remember was a slow down, and hearing my Father say, "Brake! Brake!" and all of a sudden, the car swerved into the middle of the road, and I saw a big black French car coming towards us. The last thought that went through my mind was, "Oh shit, now we are going to be too late to go to the beach", and than I blacked out. It is some how funny how our brain during emergencies switches away from the main point, and goes on to irrelevant matters, as though it does not want to face the reality.

When I came to, I was laying on the road between the two pieces of our car which had split in half. Next to me, Mom was feebly lamenting, and I could see Dad, face down in the ditch, not moving. The French car was on its side, but all in one piece. The traffic was going by slowly, without stopping; in fact, I was told it took quite some time before someone stopped and tried to help. I blacked out again, and woke up in a hospital ward with twenty or thirty beds. Next to me there was a young man whose foot had been amputated, I remember thinking, " Poor guy, he's really got it bad". Later on I learned I was in Susa, a small town near the crash site. Somebody came to my side, and asked for information on how to contact the family. I told him that my uncle Giovanni was a Jesuit, in nearby Turin, at the Institute Sociale, and that the rest of the family was in Rapallo.

After some time my uncle appeared, and when I asked him how were Dad and Mom, he told me they were being attended to in Intensive Care. In fact, Dad died at the site of the accident, and Mom shortly after her arrival at the hospital. He also told me that he was arranging for my transportation to a clinic in Turin, because I needed surgery on my shoulder and leg.

My memory of those events is strangely going from very vivid, for some happenings, to totally blurred, for others.

In Turin it turned out that my clavicle was broken, and my leg only needed stitches. I had also suffered a torn muscle, but nothing could be done for that.

After the surgery to the shoulder, an unknown Jesuit showed up at my bedside. He started asking strange questions like, "Would you give your life to save your parents?" I felt very uneasy, because I had a feeling he was about to tell me something bad. I also felt guilty, because I was not sure how to answer that question. He proceeded to tell me that my parents for sure would have given their lives to save mine, and that made me feel even more guilty. He than told me that God had taken their lives and spared mine, because He had plans for me to do something important.

I don't know who this priest was, or why he was selected to give me the news. He for sure did a horrible job, because besides making me feel very guilty for the death of my parents, he left me wondering what God had in store for me in the future. That thought stayed with me for many years, until I realized that, after all, I was not going to be a miracle maker, or a special person, and the expectations He had for me were no different from those He had for anybody else.

The rest of the summer was spent in Voltaggio where all my Romanengo uncles and aunts were staying. One by one they took me aside, and tried to make me express my feelings about what had happened. The result was quite the opposite, because I refused to share what I felt was mine, and still could not believe completely, and considered those well-meaning attempts an unwelcome intrusion. So I shut down even more, and started building a protective wall around me. When something very big happens in our lives we have the tendency to stay too close to it, and therefore we can not see the whole picture, like when you stand right at the base of a big mountain all you see is a rock wall. We are overwhelmed and unable to step back and make rational decisions. At least that's what it was like for me. I could not see the love and suffering of the rest of my family. It was just me and my pain.

At the end of the summer, all our uncles made the blessed decision that it would be better if all us children remained together in the same house, and continued our life as close as possible to the life before. I say blessed, because I feel it would have been a disaster had we been split up among the other families. Franca was put in charge of the household, and uncle Pippo was named our guardian. This decision was not very fair to Franca who, at nineteen, would have preferred to have fun and a social life, instead of having to look after her siblings, all with different needs, while she attended college at the same time. But as they say, shit happen and she was the sacrificial lamb.

Giovanni was too old to listen to her commands, and he could not wait to move out of the house. I was about to start high school, and also considered myself above her control, but she did not agree with that position, so we either scrapped or ignored each other. All the little one fell under her command, and she was a tight- fisted disciplinarian. Legend says that she instructed Signo, on weekends, to take the younger sisters to a nearby beach to watch the crowds eat ice cream. To buy one for each of them would have been too expensive and liberal.

At this time Signo appeared in our lives.

The first year after the accident a woman was hired to look after the younger brother and sisters to alleviate Franca's duties. I can't remember her name, but things did not work out and she left. Then somebody recommended Signo, a woman from a good local family who was going through financial difficulties. She was then looking after the kids of a well-to-do, but totally crazy family, and she was searching for a more sane situation. To give you an idea of how strange that family was, I'll tell you a story about the father. During the war he was kidnapped by the partisans who asked his father for a ransom. The answer they got in Genoese dialect translates to "You can keep him". The partisans returned him promptly.

To be corny, I could say that there is a silver lining to every cloud. The story of losing our parents and Signo's arrival could probably be told better, but at the end, she was a mother to my younger, sisters and a grandmother to most of the next generation.

At the end of 1956 I started high school, and studying was far from my interests. My teacher, Don Odone, was probably the best I ever had. He taught Italian, Latin, Greek and history, one after the other, for three or four consecutive periods. He knew a great deal about many cultures, which is not to be confused with erudition, which is the knowledge of facts but not the appreciation of them. And that appreciation is what Don Odone taught me. He did not care about grades or the curriculum. He would spend three periods on one subject, just explaining how that subject was connected to the history, philosophy and culture of their time. He was fascinating, but who needed to study when he did not care whether or not you were cheating on your written tests? And then the orals were a group affair. I surely did not study for the two years that he was my teacher. At the end of the second year, I had to take State exams, and that is when reality hit.

I failed Greek with a zero, Latin with a five, Math with a five and, unjustly, they failed me in Italian - I guess to make it a round number. During the summer I could have taken remedial courses and passed the three subjects in which I had the five grade, but Greek was beyond remedy, because in two years I had never opened a book on that subject. It was decided than that I should transfer to a more technical school with emphasis on economics and accounting rather than on classical languages. So I left Arecco, and went to another Catholic school, the Istituto Piccardo.

I did not care much for the change, but then I did not care much for many things at that time. Girls and sports were mostly my interests. One good thing came from that change. During that summer I had to take an integrated course in a few subjects I had never studied before, such as accounting and short hand, and which was part of the new curriculum. I remained in Rapallo under the control of my Grandmother Bice, while the rest of the family went away in August. At first, I thought that was the terrible punishment for my shortcomings. Alone with my intimidating nonna seemed a nightmare. On the contrary, it was almost fun and, I had the opportunity to know her better.

Over dinner, she told me many stories that I didn't know about my father's youth and about my uncles. She also spoke about how life was when she was growing up. For my part, during every dinner I had to explain - sometimes twice- why I was there with her.

During that time, Giovanni graduated from high school and decided that he did not want to attend college. He went to work for the ships of the Costa Line on the passenger side. He loved to play soccer, and he continued what our father had started and what had been discontinued at his death – the creation of a company soccer team. The Gruppo C started in the lower divisions, and with the years, grew to be one of the top rated semi-professional teams, with a large organization of farm teams for children six and up. He did not play for long, because in January, 1961, he married Plinia, and finally did what he had long wanted - he moved out of our house, and began his own complete family.

Costa family 1958 ?

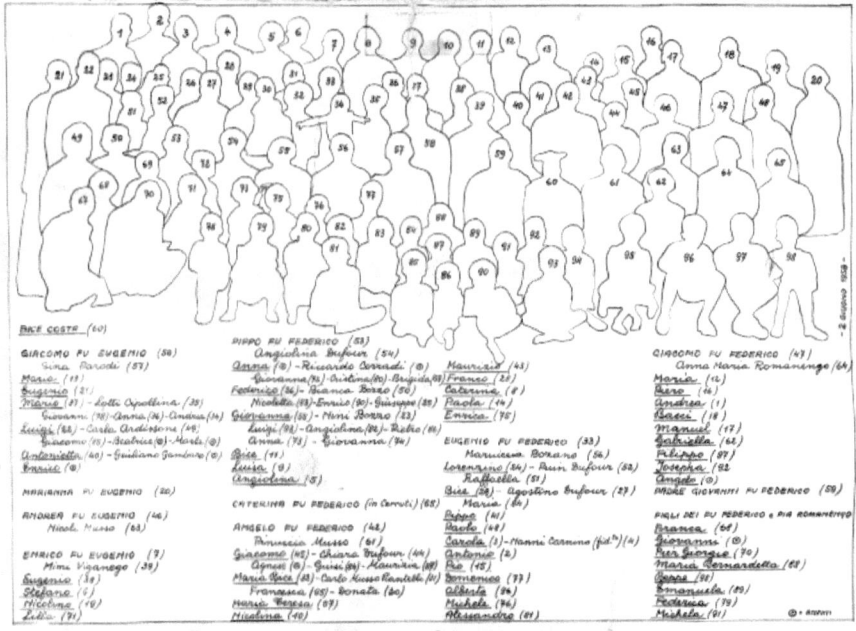

(cover) me 1945 ?

Puny & Silvia in Sestriere 1959

My mom and Franca- Giovanni in Cortina 1940 ?

Carlo and Puny in Ischia 1953

me at Loire castle 1956

Carlo and Puny wedding

My parents 1953

My parents in Rapallo 1037 ?

Paolo Romanengo, me, Giully Costa, Lorenzo R. Franca and Giovanni Alps 1953 ?

Silvia Federica and nonna
Peradotto Lanzo 1956

Costa uncles & aunts.Nonna Bice in the middle 1953 ?

Franca,Giovanni,me,Bernardetta, Beppe in Selva 1950 ?

Romanengo family L to R Francesca, my mom, Maria, Teresa, Tonino,
nonna Rosetta, Mariangela, Emanuele, Tommaso 1919?

Piero Peradotto Lanzo

Dad and mom wedding L. nonna Bice R. nonna Rosetta

Silvia and Federica with nonni
Peradotto Lanzo 1957 ?

Carl, Puny and Camilla Lanzo

Costa family 1922 in Rapallo

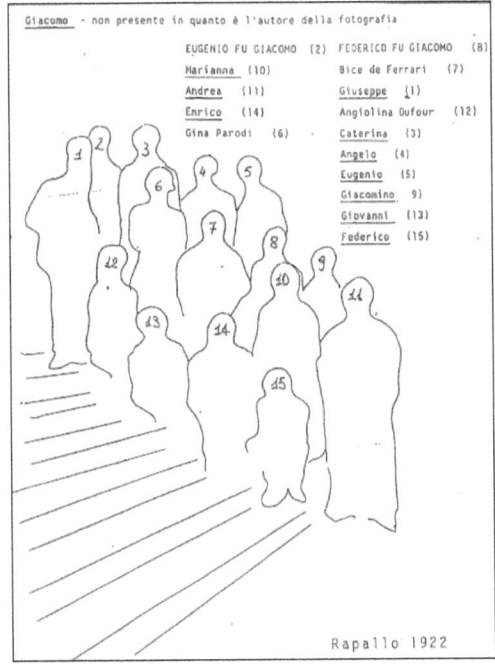

mom in her Topolino 1936 ?

our family 1955

Carlo and Silvia 1944

Camilla and Silvia 1944

9

My Brother and Sisters

It is time to step back in order to tell you about my brothers and sisters, and how the loss of our parents affected our lives.

The predominance of either the Romanengo or Costa gene separates us into two different groups. There were the outgoing, fun loving, sporting Romanengos, and the more reserved, duty-oriented, intellectual Costas. Of course, this is a generalization, but that's the way I see it, and for the record, I'm not happy to have mostly Costa genes.

In 1956, Franco and Giovanni were the older kids, I was the one in-between, and the others were the little ones. Franca was always a good student. She had just graduated from high school and was getting ready for college when our parents died in an accident. Because Franca was the oldest, she was held to a higher standard than the rest of us. I guess that is part of the reason she is a disciplinarian. She is strict with herself, and everybody else must follow suit. The severe upbringing she imposed upon our younger siblings is legendary. They were all intimidated by her, and nobody dared rebel.

She was greatly burdened by being made responsible for the family. In addition, she also had to study for her college courses. She didn't have much time for fun, or for the silly things that twenty-year olds usually do. She graduated with honors, and in 1966 married Manlio, an older man from Trieste. He was a lawyer and moved his practise to Genoa to allow Franca to stay near her siblings. It did not work out. The birth of their first daughter, Maria Benedetta, who was diagnosed with Downs Syndrome, necessitated their moving first to Milan, and then back to Trieste.

It is tragic to have a child with a handicap, and more so for Franca. She was just emerging from having to care for her younger siblings, and now her daughter needed very special attention. Her husband never accepted the situation, and didn't do much to help her. He preferred giving his attention to the two boys who were born later on.

I've always been amazed at the great job Franca did raising Maria Benedetta. In spite of her limitations, she was able to enjoy music, travel, work, and most of all, the love of the people around her. Camillo, Franca's oldest son is a prosecutor, and Federico, her youngest, is involved in the promotion of Trieste and the surrounding region. In her later years, she – like all of us – has mellowed, and let her hair down a little bit. She still holds tight to the rule that duty and sacrifice are the basis of her life. I wish she could say at least occasionally "que sera, sera".

My brother, Giovanni, on the contrary had no interest in academics and theories. His best asset is his ability to deal with people. It would be hard to find someone who didn't like him. He also has a tendency to be completely focused on what he wants, and pursues it with such enthusiasm that he is often unaware of others around him. As many older brothers are, he was my tormentor while we were growing up. He was bigger and stronger, and did not like to have a younger brother around. His excuse could be that I tattled on him to my parents occasionally, and got him into trouble. I guess I was too young to be discreet. He was much better than I in sports or other activities, and I admired his daredevil attitude. It is ironic that now he is quite sedentary, and I'm the one who's more active.

Giovanni could not wait to get away from our home, and his way of compensating for the loss of our parents was to start his own family. He married Plinia, a level-headed woman who presents a good balance to Giovanni's passions.

They had three girls in a row, and Pia, the oldest, is my Goddaughter, and is a lot like her father. After the girls, a son was born, Federico, the much-desired heir. He is also a lot like his father.

Giovanni started a soccer league, and became a mentor to many kids, giving them the opportunity to learn and play the game. His work paid off, and many of those kids made it to professional teams.

I'm close to Giovanni, despite his victimizing me when we were kids. We like to have each other's approval on important decisions. We are, however, quite different, and I have always envied his ability to relate to people, while he probably appreciates my more logical approach to problems.

His position was similar to mine when Costa reorganized. He had started a new career, and began a business that offered shore excursions to cruise lines. In time, it evolved into a complete travel company. He was successful, and I admire his ability to create a new activity without having had any prior experience in that field. He works hard, and loves what he's doing. He hasn't retired, and is not planning to do so. He's having too much fun, is full of enthusiasm, and I think would drive Plinia crazy if he stayed at home. Their two other daughters, Giovanna and Chiara, are homemakers, and busy taking care of their children. Giovanna, however, has a business on the side, and sells artisanal products to a limited clientele.

My younger siblings are Bernardetta, Beppe, Manuela, Federica, and Michela. Bernardetta was nine when our parents died, and she is probably the only one of them who has some memory of mom and dad. Growing up, she and Beppe, who is a year-and-a-half younger, teamed up. Bernardetta was the victim of my extortions when I demanded money to keep my bedroom door open at night. She and Manuela were responsible for my meeting Silvia. They were in school together, and I knew about Silvia before we actually met. I never gave them proper credit for playing Cupid.

Bernardetta was a good student – the academic genes in our family went mostly to the female side. She graduated as a lawyer, and married Fausto, one of her professors, and several years older than she is.

Fausto was a formal guy, and the story is that he proposed to her using the third person. In Italian, you only use the third person in a very formal conversation. Fausto was involved in politics, and was a member of the Christian Democratic Party – then the ruling party. This was in the seventies, during the time of the terrorist organization: the Red Brigade. A commando of the Brigade came into Fausto's classroom and shot him in the legs. It was meant as a warning to his students. This was the modus operandi of the Red Brigade: shoot a symbol of the establishment, sometimes wounding the person, other times killing him.

The Brigade also kidnapped people, demanding a ransom used to finance their organization, and I will tell you more about this later on. Their most notorious act was when they kidnapped Aldo Moro, the former head of the government and still an influential politician, and murdered him.

Back to Bernardetta, she has an ebullient personality, is easy with people, and likes to jump feet first into anything that interests her. It's amusing to have dinner with her and Giovanni and watch each one try to monopolize the conversation. Bernardetta and Fausto had two children, Valentina and Lorenzo, both very bright, and both - surprise!- lawyers.

Valentina is taking a long leave of absence to raise her children, and Lorenzo, who is a professor, seems to follow in his parents' footsteps. (Bernardetta also taught law at the university).

Like all of us, Bernardetta needed the love and stability of a mature presence. But when she grew up she also had the need to be a mentor, and to project her ideas and feelings to others. I leave it to psychologists to interpret. But I believe that all human beings are walking contradictions, and for that reason, fascinating.

Beppe, with Benardetta, was in sort of a twilght zone. They were part of the little ones, but a step ahead of the last three younger sisters. Ever since he was a child, Beppe has had a knack for telling tall stories. I remember one: he insisted that he witnessed a race between two trams trying to pass each other. Since they were on the same track it was a clear impossibility.

Beppe was my only little brother, and I wanted to be a guide for him. I guess that, like all of us, he needed a mentor from outside the immediate family. He found it in Clotilde, the girl he eventually married. They met on a long cruise to South America – surprise, surprise – it must run in the family! Being attracted to Clotilde was easy. She was pretty, a world class skier, part of the Italian Skiing Team, and she was outspoken and determined. A friend of mine- Beppe Anfossi – observed that she lived her life as though she was at the starting gate every day.

Once she retired from skiing she became passionate about car racing, and when that became too expensive, she moved on to golf, and became one of the best amateur players in Italy. My brother Beppe did not have the stamina or talent to compete with her, but he was happy to go along with whatever she wanted to do.

He moved to Turin, her home town, and started a series of very ambitious ventures, always trying to hit a home run, never content with a single or a double. He is probably the person in the family that puzzles me the most; I can't figure out which of our genes predominate in him. Beppe and Clotilde have a son, Amadeo, but I barely know Amadeo. He works for the Ducati Motorbike Racing Team, and he seems to be well-adjusted.

It is strange that I became close to my three little sisters only in our later life. It is my fault, and our age difference is no excuse. I was never part of their growing up, and Signo was their main support. It was hard for them, having no memory of our parents, especially since we – their older siblings – did not share our memories with them.

Manuela 's Godmother, our cousin Maria T, took her duties as a moral guide very seriously. Our Uncle Angelo was her father, and in her youth she had contracted a bad form of scoliosis which, at that time, was not curable. She remained short, with a hunchback. This prevented marriage, and she studied law, and became a lawyer instead. She was the first woman in the Costa family who had a job.

Maria T. visited Manuela almost daily, and usually at the least convenient time. She was intelligent, but totally inflexible, and if you let her, she would argue forever over the most unimportant subject. Manuela appreciated her love and dedication, but was embarrassed by her blunt approach to life. Emanuela is definitely a Costa, with a strong sense of duty and an interest in culture. Like me, I think she would like to have a little more Romanengo in her.

Manuela, like Federica and Michela, married her high school love. (Here again I'm sure that psychologists would have something to say about the desire to keep your first love close to you, unwilling to risk another loss.) Manuela married Paolo, and he began his life's work as an archeologist while Manuela took her degree in Biology, and then taught Math in high school. Manuela and Paolo were the most unconventional couple in our family. They traveled with very little money through Central America and South America, hitch hiking, and on local buses. When they returned to Genoa, they lived in a roof top apartment in a section of the old city that was infested with huge rats. Their neighbors were illegal immigrants and prostitutes.

They moved to New York – it was Paolo's idea to open a restaurant there - and they and two young daughters lived in Tribeca – long before it was fashionable - and once again there were rats in the neighborhood.

Manuela and Paolo have three daughters: Martina, an artist and gallery owner, Elena, who attended university in Rome, and has not yet chosen a career, and Donata, born in New York, and the first American in our family. Donata is logical and a free spirit, and for me, that is the ultimate compliment. She seems to combine an independent and adventurous side with a well-balanced and reasonable personality, and that combination is hard to find.

Federica has Giovanni's ease in dealing with people, enthusiasm, and the ability to focus on what she wants. Unlike him, however, she is extremely sensitive. I would say too sensitive for her own good, but I love her for it. She studied to be a kindergarten teacher, and taught for awhile, but then decided to move on to elementary school. She passed the necessary exams, and in the mean time, she married. The first Costa not to marry in Church. I did not attend. Not because I didn't approve, but because at the time we were living in New York, and it was not convenient for me to travel to Italy.

I was still in my self-centered phase, and I regret enormously not having made the effort to be part of that moment in her life. She has never held a grudge against me for my absence, and that makes me feel even more guilty.

Federica married Franco, a young journalist with the local paper, and they had two children: Costanza and Fedrico. Both have a feeling for social justice and a passion for the Genoa soccer team. I like them for that. Federica and Franco separated, and then divorced for a number of reasons, including the fact that Federica could not handle the idea of moving to Milan where Franco was offered a very important job. Once again, I think the death of our parents had something to do with her possible fear of parting from our family and our roots. Federica and Franco have kept a good relationship, and

I still like him. Federica is a fine teacher, working now with immigrants who are learning Italian, and I'm sure she makes a great difference in the lives of many. She loves her work, despite some bureaucratic principals, whom she says, drive her crazy. She has no qualms in forcefully opposing bureaucracy, and occasionally, her career has suffered.

Federica is the family adventurer, once again, confirming the contradiction of human nature. The woman who wouldn't move to Milan, one-hundred miles away, loves the mountains, and traveling to wild places. I envy her, because I would love to do extreme skiing, or trekking the Gobi desert, but I would never dare to do such things. Me, the one who could never resist a challenge, is settling for comfortable lodgings and resort trails. I can live with my shortcomings, but I have to acknowledge them. I discovered all that we have in common late in life, and I'm sorry it did not happen earlier.

Michela is the little one, and the only woman in the family who is not in to academics. Thank God for that, the male side of the family has company. She married young, and her wedding pictures look as though they could have been taken at her Confirmation. She is small, and along with Federica, the one who looks most like my mother. Like my mother, she does not like makeup, or dressing up. Her husband's name is also Beppe, and they are both super fans of Genoa soccer. They have two sons: Pietro and Alberto. Pietro, like his cousins, has a passion for justice as is a social worker. Alberto, much to Michela's unhappiness, is a carpenter. I have no problem with that. Everyone has his talents and aspirations, and has the right to follow them. Some years after the boys were born, Michela had a daughter, Lucy, and like all latecomers, she was doted upon. Michela is very levelheaded and proud, occasionally bordering on stubbornness. I admire her for taking responsibility for her actions, and for raising great kids. She now teaches religious education, and is the only one in the family still close to the Catholic Church. She always loved sports, but is now too busy to partake. She was an early Soccer Mom, but only Pietro gave her satisfaction in that area.

In conclusion, we all suffered because of the loss of our parents, but the weight was heavier on Franca and the young ones. Within, we all suffer from the fear of losing again what is important to us, and we all built a variety of defenses to protect us from what might happen. I think that the paragraph I read in a Tana Frech book summarize well how we felt. It wasn't affection I was after, nothing like that. What I wanted was something I belonged with, beyond any doubt or denial; someone where every glance was a guarantee, solid proof that we were stuck to each other for life. Each of us found help, comfort, and motivation from the people around us rather than from each other. That is a critique particularly of me, and the other older siblings, for not having been more available. I think, now, we have come full circle, and appreciate each other more, and are closer than ever to each other. It is sad it took us awhile to realize that while you may fall in and out of love, have friendships that may come and go, family ties last forever.

10

Meeting Silvia, Her Family, &
College

During my last school year of 1962/63, Franca decided that for the Christmas vacation she would take a cruise to North Africa, and I would go with her. I was not too excited by the idea because I was flirting with a girl, and school vacations were a good opportunity to spend time together. My friend Beppe Anfossi, and my cousin Franco were also going on the cruise, and friends were more important than dates. So I went along.

From my sisters, Bernardetta and Manuela, I learned that a girl who went to school with them, Silvia Vaccari, and who had recently moved across the street from us, would also be going on the cruise with her mother. Manuela was a classmate of Federica, her younger sister. I knew of Silvia, but we didn't hang around with the same friends.

There were not too many young people aboard ship, so it was natural to spend time with those few who were there. There was a girl from Milan exhibiting leather mini skirts and wearing heavy makeup, and she looked like a possibility. My friend Beppe, allied with Silvia, made fun of my taste and choice, but they were willing to help me in my endeavor. Camaraderie, that's how it started.

On December 31st we were in Egypt, and took a flight to Luxor to visit the Valley of the Kings and the Temple of Karnak. On the return, one of the chartered planes broke down, and there was a request for volunteers who would stay back, and wait for another plane. All the young people responded, and we sat in the lobby of an old Victorian hotel facing the Nile, chatting about all and nothing. Talking to Silvia, we began to think that this was something more than camaraderie. We lived on the same street, but had to go to a different continent to find each other. Sounds corny, huh?

Upon our return to Genoa, at first with Beppe Anfossi as a chaperone, we started dating. Silvia's mother, Puny, liked me, so she did not place any obstacle in our path. I was welcome to go to their house to watch television; we did not have a TV in our house because Franca deemed it too much of a distraction to studying and education in general. I think we were quite unique in that matter, but then, no one dared challenge Franca's rules. We kept dating through the winter and spring, until we both graduated from high school. We were two years apart, but I had lost one year when I switched schools, and Silvia's language school was one year shorter.

Silvia did not have much interest in arts or sports. Her taste in music, by her own admission, was super cheesy. She had, however, two great assets: she was funny and outgoing, and had great practical sense. To me, super-introverted and dark, her sunny disposition was enchanting. She taught me to loosen up, and I finally started to open to other people without fear of being hurt. Her practical sense was a good balance to my idealistic view of life. She was fearful but courageous, and that is not a contradiction. She was afraid of many things, but she faced them without running away.

When summer arrived she visited me in Rapallo, and with my cousins, we went out in the infamous Cigno, the boat of no return, for a swim. As usual, on the way back, the engine refused to start, and as a consequence we were half an hour late for lunch at home. There we found an icy Franca, who without raising the tone of her voice, showed her contempt for the delay.

I thought that would be the end of our relationship. Silvia, fortunately, albeit quite impressed, managed to see a funny side to the situation. In the future, she tried to steer clear of Franca whenever she could, and the memory of this story resurfaced many times in the future, whenever we faced embarrassing situations.

Let us open a parenthesis to learn more about the Vaccaris.

Carlo was the father. He was an engineer, had a logical personality, and was more interested in facts than people. He was born in Ponzano, near the Ligurian Tuscan border, where his family had a high-quality tile factory. They made the best tiles in Italy, but they were also quite expensive. In the seventies, the competition from cheaper, lower quality products became too much for them, and the company went bankrupt. Carlo was a quiet man, with curly blond hair and blue eyes. During the war, he served on the Greek front as an artillery officer. He loved sailing, and as a young man, owned a beautiful sailboat that played a big role in getting the attention of Puny. The boat was bombed by planes, and sank during the war. He never bought a new one, and preferred to sail on yachts that belonged to friends. He was welcomed on many regattas because of his skill. He did not like to socialize, and tried as much as possible to avoid the parties that Puny loved. He had twin sisters, Pia and Luisa. They were called the mini-aunts because they did not reach five feet in height. They both married lawyers, and had children around the same age as Silvia.

One of them, Beppe Vernetti, was in my school, and we were in the same grade. Beppe was a very good student and very diligent. He never allowed me to copy his work when I tried to cheat during a test. I never held that against him, because sometimes I was so bad, that not even copying would have helped. I got back at him later on when he came with us skiing, or on other trips, before we married. Silvia and I played all sorts of practical jokes on him, and he took it all with good humor. And it was not to get even. He was so proper and neat that you could not help making fun of him.

Carlo would mostly spend his vacations with Federica, while Puny went somewhere with Silvia - as she did on the cruise where we met. Carlo also loved soccer, and we went to the stadium together many time. I liked the man. Federica was Silvia's little sister, and physically looked like her father, with blue eyes and blond curly hair. She was in the same grade as my sister Manuela, and I knew her before I met Silvia, because Federica would come to our house to study with Manuela. She also did not have a great interest in a social life, and preferred small groups to large events. She had a determined character, just short of stubbornness. I remember her, one evening in Lanzo, having an argument with her grandfather Silvio. She punched him in the stomach, and was sent away from the dining table when she wouldn't stop arguing. Her vocabulary was also suspect. Once she took offence when Silvia said that her dress looked like that of a belly dancer. The Italian word for "belly dancer" sounds similar to the word for "prostitute" and she confused the two. Puny made the same mistake, and scolded Silvia for insulting her sister.

Puny was born in Turin. Her family, the Peradottos, originally came from the country. Her father, Silvio, was the director of a tannery, but his older brother, Tunin, still lived on the farm when Silvia and I got engaged. Tunin was a peculiar guy who resented the social success of his two brothers, and was always involved in weird deals. During the war, while the house in Lanzo was occupied by German troops, he bought a stock of rifles on the black market with the idea of reselling them to the partisans. He did not have any better idea than storing them in his brother's villa with German soldiers all around. Had the rifles been found, executing part of the family would have been a likely probability. Silvio's other brother, Nanni, had only one son, Franco. Franco was a bon vivant who loved the social life. He played polo, a quite elitist sport even then, and never got married.

This, coupled with the fact that Piero and Camilla did not have children, resulted in the extinction of the name Peradotto. A fact that always saddened the family. Silvio, in 1939 decided to go into business for himself, and left the tannery. On March 8th, " For the grace of God and the will of the Nation and the graciousness of the King of Italy and Emperor of Ethiopia", as it reads in the incorporation papers, FIMIT was founded. The company manufactured sound insulation material at Turin's outskirts. The big turning point for the company happened in 1950, when FIMIT signed an agreement with FIAT, the largest carmaker in Italy, to supply panels for the booming economy car market. Their success was huge and swift, and Silvio's son Piero provided the leadership for the expansion. Right after graduating from college Piero married Camilla Botto, the only daughter of a family from Biella which manufactured textiles. Camilla's father, Albino, died early, and her mother Deli then married Mario Alasonatti, and they moved to Monte Carlo. He was a true gentleman in the style of Edward, Prince of Wales, always perfectly dressed for any occasion, and driving a Rolls Royce. He escorted Puny on many cruises around the world. She was an incredible character. Sharp as a tack even in her later years. She could care less for formalities or propriety. She loved to gamble at the casino, but she was too down to earth to get herself into trouble. Deli and Puny had major clashes of personality on how to conduct social life in the Principality of Monaco.

I liked Camilla a lot, she was an anglophile like my mother, and she had a sly sense of humor that I enjoyed. She had, in Piero, a husband with a powerful personality, but she managed, much to Puny's envy, to make him do whatever she wanted, or almost that. She had the practical sense of her mother, and a directness in relationships that I approve of.

Now back to Puny. In her youth she was a sort of tomboy, with an appreciation for fashion. Her mother, Rosalin, was very strict with her, while Silvio allowed her everything. One day while her mother had friends over for a card game, Puny decided to dress herself in feathers taken from the hats of the guests. At the time, a lady could not go out without wearing such a hat. Puny cut off all the feathers and proceeded with her creation. Another time she had to attend a funeral, and her mother did not have the time to take her shopping to buy shoes for the occasion so she went with a maid. Puny had long wanted semi- high heels, and her mother had said she was too young for them. Sure enough, that day she bought those shoes. In response her mother cut the heels, and she was forced to go around with her toes pointing up.

The Peradottos vacationed on the Ligurian Riviera, and one summer she met Carlo, and was invited to go sailing. They say that the opposites attract, and this was as true for them as - to a certain extent - it was for me and Silvia. Puny's ebullience, and easiness in relating to people, was a counter balance to Carlo's quiet and introverted personality. They married in Lanzo, in 1943, during the war, and about one year later Silvia was born. During their engagement, Carlo visited Lanzo, making the trip from Genoa on a bike, pedaling for close to one-hundred and fifty miles each way. On the way, he had to negotiate road blocks and bombing. To be in love was a demanding task in those years. After the war Puny moved to Genoa, but she never liked the reserved, and some how provincial, atmosphere of the city. It did not help that her in-laws were super conservative. She was greatly criticized - for example – because she rode a Vespa scooter around town, and her father had to make a trip to Genoa to iron things out between the families. Social life, proper etiquette and elegance were her main interests, all things that Carlo could not be talked into. Ankle or mid-calf socks and short sleeved shirts were anathema to Puny, and so was wearing brown or tan shoes after seven PM; Carlo complied with a grudge.

Silvia was followed three years later by a sister, Federica. It looked like the parents' genes were split evenly: Silvia got Puny's, and Federica, blond with blue eyes, got Carlo's. Silvia dealt easily with people, and had an airy personality. Federica exhibited the more quiet, and reasoning approach to life of Carlo. The genes were noticeable also in school results. Federica was a good student, but was too nervous to score well on exams. Silvia couldn't care less, and often spent the last semester of each school year living at a convent, in a desperate attempt to catch up with the rest of her class. The measure was also meant as punishment, but she liked the communal life at the convent school, and was not too bothered by loss of freedom. What did bother her was the obligation of spending one month each summer in Lanzo. She hated the way her grandmother Rosalin, and her uncle Piero, criticized Puny for the way she raised her daughters, and the fact that Puny never rebelled. That dislike of Piero continued in later life. She also found the place boring, with few things to do for fun. She resented the quiet demanded by the afternoon naps of the adults, and she missed the friends left at the beach in Genoa. Lanzo, however, was a must part of her vacation.

When the Vaccari's tile company went bankrupt, the banks became interested in the private property of the owners. Puny took that opportunity to move to Monte Carlo, where social life is a "raison d'etre". Her second life started then. She gave and attended dinner parties and balls. She would change clothes three times a day for different occasions, and loved it. She worked very hard to be the perfect hostess. She made an effort to have everything perfect, including the way she dressed, and how she decorated her house. But who am I to criticize? I tend to put a lot of work into the way I dress, and how my house is decorated, all to create an opposite disorderly, casual look that is even more difficult to achieve. I don't know who is more snob. Anyway, Puny never regretted being in Monaco. Carlo, however, went to Turin, and worked for FIMIT. A few years later he developed a very painful form of bone cancer. I don't remember ever hearing him complain, and he endured his illness with great dignity, almost apologizing for the inconvenience he was creating for his family.

Lets go back to 1963. At the end of the summer, before starting college, I went to London for two months to improve my limited English. Silvia went to Paris for three months to a finishing cum cooking school. The attendees were supposed to learn proper social skills as well as haute cuisine. The program ended with a debutante's ball. After that, Silvia planned to go to London in January for three months, to learn English. We were a little concerned about what the separation could do to our relationship, but we were still interested in each other when we met again in the spring. My major cheerleader was Puny, she liked me in spite of my lack of social skills and ambitions, traits that on the contrary, were appreciated by Silvia.

Meanwhile, I started college at the University of Economics. In Italy, the universities are all urban and do not offer housing facilities. It is, therefore, normal to attend college in your hometown and to live at home.

More than attending classes, I was giving myself an education in the movies. With a couple of friends, we would see up to three movies a day, visiting all the art houses to see the old classics, and, of course, the contemporary films as well. I also started to train with my brother Giovanni's soccer team, and played with the second team. I mostly was called from the bench, but it was enough for me to be part of the group.

It was fun, but the academic results were not good, and I limped along for a couple of years, passing half the necessary courses. Silvia, in the mean time, studied to be a translator, and occasionally worked for trade shows where a French or English hostess was needed. Our relationship was becoming stronger, and more serious, and we started thinking about getting married. To speed things up, I decided to serve my time in the army immediately – at that time it was an obligation - rather than waiting for the end of college. I intended to keep studying at the same time, but I knew that I was kidding myself trying to do that. In fact, that year I passed only three courses. At the end, the inevitable happened: I did not finish college, and started working in order to get married. I regret my decision, not so much because I miss what I did not learn, but because I did not have the integrity to finish what I had started.

11

The Army, Work and Marriage

My brother Giovanni had friends at the army district that helped his soccer players by assigning them to Genoa, or nearby, so that they were available to continue to play for his team. He was supposed to extend the same treatment to me. It was some how a shock when my papers arrived, and I learned that I was assigned instead to Barletta, a small town in the far away southern region of Puglia. Least to say I was pissed, but in life you never know, the long run is more important than the short. I had a great experience meeting people I would never have met had I remained in the protected local environment. It was also fun. I was in great shape, and my only concern was to make myself inconspicuous, and avoid all the military detail that I could.

I will be always grateful to Puny who escorted Silvia to that totally unglamorous far away place for a quick visit. She really must have liked me.

From Barletta, I was reassigned to Naples Communication School. There we learned how to operate radio equipment, and starved because the food was inedible. There, with the help of a new friend, Giuseppe, a law student, we convinced our Captain that we both were architectural students, and could prepare a drawing for a house he wanted to have built in a nearby sea resort. We told him we had access to a studio, where after hours we could work on it. He was convinced enough to issue us liberty passes for every night until midnight. In the army, at the time, you were allowed off base only few times a week, and normally you had to be back by nine P.M.

I used those evenings mostly to eat, and to take showers. At the base you could shower once a week, and the water was always cold. The whole thing could have had an ugly ending if we did not show some results. Fortunately, Giuseppe lived nearby, and had a friend who was a genuine architect, and the drawings were presented to the Captain's satisfaction. I'm amazed now how irresponsible I was then.

After graduation from Communication School, I was supposed to go back to Barletta, but Franca's future husband, Manlio, was more reliable than my brother Giovanni, and he managed to have me transferred to Florence. I've never been fond of him, but that was a huge favor that he did for me. From Florence, it was easy to get home with a pass meant for taking exams. Most of all, nine months spent in that beautiful city and its surrounding hills was an unforgettable experience. I had my own car - which I was not supposed to drive while in the army - and Silvia and I would meet half way in Pisa, and spend the day together during weekends.

The army base was very small, and our company consisted of only one-hundred men, all friends, covering for each other when it was needed. I managed to get into the office that organized the war games that happened twice a week, as well as the weekly march. The war games consisted of spreading the men out on the hills around the city; we had short wave radios, and exchanged messages to prove that we were really there, and had done our job. I was in charge of preparing the messages, and everyone knew ahead of time what they were. All they had to do was to copy them, and enjoy the day. It was a waste of time, but we had a great deal of fun. The itinerary of the weekly march always included some historical or artistic landmark off the beaten track, and I was able to visit places I would never have seen otherwise. After my honorable discharge I started working.

For the Costa males there were two options: Seminary or the Costa office. The Costa women, on the other hand, were meant to be housewives, and all the older women did just that. The first one to have a career outside the home was Maria T., who became a lawyer. After her, others became teachers. None of the women worked for the Costa Company, and that was a clear injustice .

It never occurred to me to consider any other option. That's the way it was: we knew discipline and obedience. At times, I wonder if I would have been better off choosing another career, but I'm not lying when I say I'm happy with what I did.

In the mean time, I proposed to Silvia, and had the awkward duty of asking for her hand from Carlo, her father. Fortunately, the man was less into the protocol than I was, we had few laughs, and he gave us his blessing.

I would have liked to work in the passenger division of the company, as had my dad and Giovanni, but it was decided that I would go into the oil division, and related businesses. I was disappointed, but had no say in the matter. What interested me in the oil division was the marketing of the various brands, and guess what? I did not get that either. I ended up working under my cousin Lorenzo in the bulk buying and selling of products, as well as related services.

Obedience to one's elders was a duty and a virtue, or so I was told, and there I was, against my best instincts, going along with that philosophy. Lorenzo was quite my opposite. He had little cultural interests, and was an opinionated doer with a big appetite for the material aspects of life. I learned a lot from him, though I did not share many of his interests.

He trusted me, and gave me responsibilities in the corporate culture where decisions were usually left to our seniors. He taught me to work hard, but also to give myself time for fun, and to unwind. He was the best mentor I could have hoped for. Here again, short term disappointment in life gave me room for long term success.

For the first year I was left on my own. I was told to spend time in the factory, and learn the production /distribution cycle. I also sat at a desk across from Lorenzo, seeing the way he worked. I felt I was wasting time, but in some unstructured way I learned.

At the end of that year of training Silvia and I got married. The date: June 10th, 1967, and the place: the same church where I was baptized. Puny, in charge of logistics, outdid herself. The church decorations and flowers were incredible, and so was the setting at the hotel where we had the reception. It also helped that the weather was sunny and mild. We spent our honeymoon touring my dream country: the USA. It was our first time in New York, and we were in awe of the city. While we were visiting Washington Square someone pinched Silvia's behind, something I would have expected in Rome, but not there. She considered that a compliment and funny. I was not thrilled but laughed.

We went afterwards to San Francisco, at the time "The City of Flowers". It was June, 1967, the "Summer of Love" and we were unaware of all that was going on. There, for the first time, I drove an automatic shift, and almost ended our marriage. Instead of leaving the gear on D and drive, I kept shifting as I would with a manual transmission. The problem was that every time I shifted, I was pushing the brake, thinking it was the clutch. The sudden stops threw Silvia into the windshield a few times before she gave me an ultimatum. I eventually learned to drive properly on the way to Sausalito, Carmel, Yosemite, L.A., Death Valley and Las Vegas. In Italy, cars did not have air conditioning, so it did not occur to me to reserve a car with it. The drive through the desert was epic, and when we reached the hotel in Vegas, we looked more like survivors than normal tourists. I was required to pre-pay the room when we checked in. After that, we visited New Orleans, ate Cajun food, and listened to jazz at night. We then flew to Miami for a Trans-Atlantic trip to Genoa, on the Federico C. I was hooked, America was were I wanted to be.

During the first years of our marriage was when "parocchietta" started. A literal translation of "parocchietta" is a little church congregation. We used the term for a group of male friends who grew up together, attended the same schools, and spent the nights doing the things boys do. Now that our dates had become fiancées or wives, we enjoyed more conventional activities, such as movies and dinners, going to a night club, or meeting in somebody's house for conversation and card games - a lot of card games. The problem was that no weekend went by without getting together, and if someone wanted to do something with other people it was regarded as treason.

The parocchietta still exists, albeit with less stringent rules, and every time I go back to Genoa I love to spend an evening with the same friends, so I can catch up with our lives.

12

Work

The working day started around 8.30 A.M. in the "sala posta". Literally translated it means "mail room", where all company mail was delivered and sorted. In reality, it was the place where corporate policies were decided. "The Giacomo Costa Fu Andera S.N.C.", the holding company of the group, was unique. Its partners were brothers and cousins, all with equal ownership, and personally liable for the company. All had single signature privilege that was binding to all the others.

The structure that normally is used only in small family operations was used for this multi-national corporation. No one had a title, just responsibility for a job, and was required to report to all the others. Investment opportunities were discussed informally in the "sala posta" where everyone congregated before going to their desks. It was more a time of sharing information rather than decision making, because it was assumed that whoever was making the proposal had his facts straight. The informal leader was Angelo, and he had the last say, but he rarely opposed a project. It was a system that required complete trust and willingness to accommodate the requests of others. The abhorred Socialist and Fascist philosophies, in a sense were, used to run the company.

That system worked well for a long time, but eventually, was the downfall of the corporation. In order to accommodate every department's desire to expand, the company became over leveraged, and the load of the interest was too much for a healthy balance sheet.

The "sala posta " was also the place for keeping up to date with the family. Weddings, births, vacations, hobbies and illness, all were part of the morning conversation. Around nine, everyone collected his mail and telexes and headed for his desk.

On normal days, around 1.00 PM, we would go home for lunch, and return at 2.30 or so, and stay until 7.00 P.M. For a long time, we worked on Saturday mornings, but that changed in the early eighties.

After my year of looking around, I was given the responsibility for the fleet of trucks that delivered bulk, or packaged oil, to the clients or our warehouses. We had about fifteen aging semis and tankers and twenty unionized drivers. We were also renting trucks from outside sources when they were needed.

It is very hard to control the productivity of a driver on the road. The excuses for traffic, weather, snags at loading or unloading, and other reasons for delay, are easy to make, and hard to challenge. The maintenance costs were also very high. Our in-house distribution was more expensive than when we worked with outside suppliers. Strong unions made it impossible to get rid of the department.

During the year I spent looking around the factories, I had the opportunity to know all our drivers, and establish personal relationships with them. I think I was seen more like a normal guy rather than a member of management. Therefore, when I proposed selling the fleet to the drivers at a good price, and also promised to rent the fleet back from them – and at the same price we were paying outside sources - I had credibility, and they accepted.

At the end, it was a rare win- win proposition. We dramatically reduced our distribution costs, and the drivers, working as independent contractors, made more money than before.

In about one year I managed to work myself out of my job. What next? During that year I had developed good relations with our bulk clients, arranging the schedule of deliveries to suit them. I helped them when they needed something in a hurry, and I always gave them reliable information. Here again, I developed credibility, and I really enjoyed working with them. After the truck's fleet, I was given the responsibility for the bulk sales of seed oil.

Some of our buyers in the south were also olive oil traders, and eager to sell their product to us. I started, with the blessing of Lorenzo, to combine sales and purchases, and got involved in the oil trade. In the south of Italy, hospitality is sacred, and has rules. You can't escape those rituals. When I was visiting, it was impossible to refuse one or two cups of espresso necessary just to start the conversation. At the end of the day I was shaking from the excess of caffeine, and spent lots of sleepless nights. Food also played a large part, and when I visited four or five clients daily, indigestion was always a possibility.

On the positive side our sales grew, and I was developing a good reputation with my uncles.

It is funny that while I'm considered an introvert I love to deal with people, and can interact with them like an extroverted salesman. Human nature is full of contradictions, and that's why it is so fascinating.

I think my introverted side comes from the fact that I have a problem in verbalizing an abstract concept unless I really work at it. My extroverted side is probably due to my enthusiasm and curiosity, and my empathy for other human beings.

It should be noted, also, that when I grew up our heroes were characters like James Dean, dark underdogs in need of love. It was a good tactic to pick up girls.

13

Our Family

During the first two years of our marriage we lived in a great little house. In Genoa, there is a fishermen's village called Boccadasse, that literally means "ass mouth", like the shape of the bay it surrounds. It is an enclave, with the city growing around it. The majority of the narrow streets are too small for cars. Our house was one of the few new ones, and was built by a developer who added an annex for possible future needs. In the meantime, we were renting it.

The house was on a cliff above the sea, and a narrow path went down to a small private pebble beach. One of our neighbors fished right from his deck, and we could have done the same from ours. It was extremely romantic and unique. I bought a moped to commute to the office and beat the traffic. We had only one car then, a sporty two seater that was a wedding present from Silvia's dad, Carlo. Silvia needed the car during the day, because the house was rather isolated.

After about two years, our landlord's business was not doing well, and he offered us the house for thirty-six million lire or what would have been approximately fifty-thousand dollars at that time. I wanted to buy, but had no experience in real estate, so I my cousin Emanuele Romanengo for advice. He was working in that field. He told me the price was astronomical, and I regretfully passed on the opportunity. Instead, we bought an old attic right in the center of town, just a few minutes walk from the office. We paid the equivalent of forty-thousand. It was larger, and practical, but not as romantic.

We did not want children right away, but after two years Silvia started to think we had a problem conceiving. Fertility clinics did not exist at the time, but her gynecologist assured us there was nothing wrong. Nevertheless, Mom was getting nervous, and on the advice of a family friend she decided to go to a spa which had mud and water, among other benefits, which were said to induce fertility. The name of the town and the spa is Salso Maggiore, an art deco place better known for being the home of the Miss Italia Pageant.

I still don't believe that the mud and water did it, but not long after that treatment, Silvia became pregnant, and that's a fact. Maybe tales from old midwives carry some truth.

In June 1970, the World Cup was played in Mexico, and the whole nation was glued to TV sets every night. Italy made it to the semifinals, and on June 17th played against Germany; even today, the game is considered one of the most exciting in the history of soccer. Italy won 4 to 3 in overtime.

After the game, all of Genoa invaded the streets in the center of town to celebrate, and traffic was paralyzed. Silvia was supposed to have the baby around that time, but fortunately nothing happened that night. It would have been impossible to drive to the hospital from our house with all that going on.

The finals between Italy and Brazil was scheduled for June 20[th,] and we were afraid of being stuck in a similar situation. Fortunately, Allegra was smart enough to arrive on the 19th - a good decision - because though Italy lost, the crowd paralyzed the center of the city anyway.

Silvia and I had never taken care of babies, and had no one to show us what to do. The culture of our families, at that time, was to delegate babies and their needs to nannies. I don't remember my father ever being involved in diaper changing, and my Mom did that rarely. She did, however, breast-feed all of us. A similar situation was true on the Vaccari side. We than decided to hire a young woman who had just graduated from a famous children's nursing school in Trento. Elisabetta was physically small, but huge in character. She bossed us around, employing all the theories she had learned – down to the last comma. We were allowed to pick up Allegra only at certain times of the day, and only for a limited time. No exceptions were allowed to the routine. She was pleasantly firm but quite a Nazi. Silvia felt she was missing something, because she was deprived of the daily chores needed for raising her baby. We were happy, when at Paolo's birth, fifteen months later, Elisabetta announced that her school had offered her a position there.

She was replaced by Marilena, a nice, laid back, chubby girl, who helped without being intrusive. Marilena was with us until Alberto was ten months old, and was replaced by the "ina cattiva", (mean nanny), I can't remember her real name. She came to us highly recommended by some of Puny's friends. She had worked for some noble family, and we had again a small woman, big on discipline. Unlike Elisabetta, however, she was not pleasant. I fired her for slapping Allegra hard for some minor infraction. It must be noted that was not the first episode of physical discipline. That was the end of the nannies in our family.

Three years after Paolo, Alberto arrived, and we had our first health scare with the children when we had to hospitalize him. He had contracted a bad flu, and was throwing up all the fluid we were trying to give him, and getting severely dehydrated. Some thirty years before, a cousin of mine died from the same condition. At the hospital, Alberto was put on an IV, and the needle was inserted in his head. It really looked scary to me. Fortunately, in a couple of days all was back to normal, and we went home. We had another scare when Paolo ate a box of fruit flavored baby aspirin. We had to go to the emergency room and have his stomach pumped. Because of that, for a while, he had a very delicate digestion. He lived mostly on carrot puree, and ice cream was forbidden. As a consequence, no one in the family ate ice cream. Other than that, we were fortunate, and survived without possible disasters, such as the time Paolo threw a golf ball from our deck down into the busiest street in the city and did not kill anyone. Another time, Allegra, feeling unappreciated, left the house carrying her doll's suitcase and announced she was moving out. She halted her departure to talk to the doorman, and returned after a little while, complaining because we did not try to stop her. She managed, however, to steal coins from a blind beggar. Mom was very embarrassed when she had to return them and apologize. Paolo had a sort of security blanket in a fluffy stuffed dog, and he could not go to sleep without it. One day that stuffed dog was so smelly and dirty that Mom decided to wash it. Strangely enough, without its odor, it lost its appeal, and Paolo just stopped using it. Al had his "golly", a blue blanket that endured much washing, and was then replaced with a yellow one, before he decided he did not need a "golly" anymore. Allegra, I guess, was tougher, because she never needed these security symbols. She was, however, in need of a bedtime story to be told in the dark until she fell asleep.

14

A Bad Time

At the office my career was proceeding brilliantly, and all that success turned me into quite a self centered idiot. My involvement with purchases extended to seed oil grains: mostly soybeans and peanuts. To be clear, Lorenzo was in charge of that department, but more and more he involved me in the process.

The American grain companies who were our suppliers invited me to visit their facilities in the USA and Brazil, and that's when I learned how most of the other manufacturers worked.

The Costa oil philosophy - from the very beginning - was to speculate. The founders of Costa were merchants. They bought oil when they felt the market was low, and held it for resale later on. The advent of the factories added a different dimension to the procedure. Now a constant supply of raw material was needed to keep the equipment working. The problem was partially solved by introducing packaged oil for distribution through stores. A brand created a predictable outflow of product, with prices less sensitive to market fluctuations. The capacity of the factories, however, well exceeded the need for the brands, and the production of olive and seed oil generated a large amount of sub-products that needed to be sold. The bulk sales that I was involved in with Lorenzo, went from olein, used in soap making, to lecithin, for cosmetics and ice cream. Other products were soybean and peanut meal for animal feed, and that was all in addition to the vegetable oils.

The market for these commodities was highly volatile. That meant that we were speculating on almost 70% of the value of a 22,000 ton seed oil grain shipment which was needed to keep just one of our factories in production for one month. Every time we made a purchase we were at risk.

In the USA, the manufacturers used the Chicago Mercantile Exchange to buy or sell grain, oil and meal, as a hedge against their actual physical transactions. These operations determined a production margin without the risk of speculation. In Italy, we did not have an institution like the Chicago Mercantile Exchange. I thought, however, to use a similar approach: selling long term oil and meal contracts to our clients every time we decided to make a purchase. When the industrial margin was high, we did transactions well into the future.

The system worked very well, and we were able to lock in higher profits.

What I did not consider was that, after some years, when the market had a huge down turn, our clients would default on their contracts, while we were committed to our purchases. That happened, however, after I left the oil division for the shipping division, and that's another story. In those prosperous years I was a big shot, and felt I was above the rest, a "master of the universe" to quote the book "Bonfire of the Vanities". Instead, I was just an ordinary presumptuous youth with an inflated ego. I was too frequently arrogant, using more sarcasm than irony in dealing with people. I played golf and cards for high stakes. I was self- centered, all in all, not a nice guy, and that was probably reflected in the way I dealt with the family.

It was a good thing that the company decided to send some of the family to look after the American operations that were growing in an unstructured way. Two volunteers who would be willing to live for a few years in the USA were needed.

I had no experience in shipping, and very little in administration, but the idea of going to the country of my dreams was too good to pass up. Besides, my inflated ego made me over-confident. I said I was available to go. Silvia had mixed feelings about going, but Puny was happy to have a daughter living in New York. It was very high society and that trumped her fear of flying.

My cousin Emanuele and I were selected. I had responsibility for the cruise division, and he was in charge of developing other business opportunities.

15

Moving to America

My change of work brought a new boss, my cousin Giacomo, called the Third, because we had already two uncles with that name. He was my Godfather and a son of Angelo. We had different approach on how to work, and never reached the symbiosis I had with Lorenzo.

I was very happy to be selected to direct Costa Cruise USA, but in retrospect, it was a terrible idea from business a point of view.

The philosophy behind it was that if you are a good manager you can apply your skills to any trade. That might be true in a vacuum, but in real life the technical knowledge and the network of human contacts you develop in one field are more important than your theoretical abilities. This was in addition to learning and adjusting to a different culture and language. I had to do all that while I had the responsibility of running the company. I, therefore, made mistakes, and that was a good lesson in humility. What I got right was the perception that our company was loosing market share and image because of its refusal to recognize that the competition was doing a better job in serving the needs of the public. All our hotel management was Italian, accustomed to catering to Europeans, and the service was, more or less, the same for the cruises in the Mediterranean as for those in the Caribbean. However, what worked in the Mediterranean did not necessarily working over here. The service managers could not accept those differences, and never admitted that their expertise did not work with American clients. In addition, our ships were getting older, and did not offer the amenities of new vessels.

I probably did a poor job of selling those arguments to the head office in Genoa, because they were not accepted for quite some time, and the feeling was that our product was better than those of our competitors. Eventually,

Genoa understood that we needed to change, but by then I was not there, because I had started my own company.

In November of 1976 I arrived in the States for an for a period I was going back and for. I was normally spending three or four weeks here and than back to Italy for one or two weeks. It was hard to live away from family and friends, but the new work was fascinating, and I was discovering the country of my dreams.

During those months a traumatic event happened. Emanuele's brother, Piero, was kidnapped by the Red brigade. He was held prisoner, mostly blind folded and handcuffed, for four or five months, before a ransom was paid, and he was freed. During that peroid, the terrorists threatened to kidnap someone else if the family did not speed up the negotiations. We all lived in anxiety, and being away from my family was even harder. Finally, the matter was over, but I was happy to have my children out of the country, because kidnappings were still frequent.

In August 1977, we moved to Bronxville, and the family's adjustment to the new life started. Allegra was in first grade, Paolo in kindergarten, and Al in nursery school, where he made a friend with a "blue face", his first encounter with people of a different race.

Bronxville in those days was mainly a WASP community, and we were among the first foreigners to move there. We were not the only ones, because besides many Asian families, during the next two years three or four Italian families moved in. The first day of school was hard, especially for Paolo who cried his heart out, because he did not want his mom to leave him there. The same scene was repeated the following year, but eventually he survived. Academically, the adjustment took a little time, because we could not help the children properly at home, and it was decided to have Allegra and Paolo repeat grades to ease their transition to the new life. It seemed hard to lose the friends they had made during that first year, but in the long run I don't think they were scarred by our decision, and school was not too much of a struggle after that. They both made new friends, and are still close to them today.

Mom had the hardest job. I had my hands full with the office, and had opportunity to meet many new people. You had your hands full with school, and made friends. She was alone at home, and had to deal with our problems when we were back at home. To compensate, she involved herself in the school system as a class mother, head of the international mothers group, Brownies and Cub Scouts Den Mother, and any other area where she could help. Through the school she was able to make new friends, and life became easier for her as well.

We were not too surprised that Allegra and Paolo wanted to be like everyone else. That meant their Italian style of clothing, food, and habits, had to change to conform to that of their friends. Al was more faithful to his origin, at least as far as food was concerned, he never gave up his pasta or pesto sauce. He, however, liked the black leather jacket of Fonzy in "Happy Days", and we had to buy it for him. As said we were not surprised, and understood your reason, but we were somehow saddened by your lost individuality.

In the meantime, as if we had not enough changes to adjust to, we had a new entity in our family. Batufolo was our first dog, and we were not ready for him. To make the idea of the move to America more acceptable to Allegra, she was promised a puppy dog upon arrival. Not many weeks passed before she claimed what had been promised. She opted for a Cairn Terrier, the first dog she saw at the pet store, and we had no idea what we were getting into. Poor Batufolo, he was mostly confined to the basement because we did not know how to house train him. No wonder he had a tendency to run away. Once he was away for three days. He was our guinea pig for the future dog we got.

In the summer we went back to Europe for our vacation. Puny had the very good idea to buy a villa near Monte Carlo, so that her two daughters and grandchildren could spend time together and with her. La Colmianne was perched on a bluff in the middle of Cap Martin Bay, and the view was spectacular. We spent part of our summer at the Beach Club, with celebrities and the jet set, and I'm sure our children did not realize how privileged was the life they were living. Water skiing with Princess Stefanie, and bathing in the pool with Roger Moore - AKA James Bond - does not happen to everyone. With us were Francesca and Giacomo, the children of Federica, who had married Mauro, a young man from Genoa.

They had moved to Torino because zio Piero, without children, wanted some family member there to continue his work. The whole thing did not work out. Mauro was opposed by the old management of FIMIT, they were probably jealous of his designated heir position, and decided to resign. For this, as well as other reasons, his relationship with Federica deteriorated. After few separations, they decided to get a divorce. Some years later, there was a possibility for me to go to Torino and work for FIMIT, but Silvia strongly opposed that move, and she was right. I don't think I would have fit in. During the Colmianne years, however, all was rosy, and the summer spent with the children's cousins forged a friendship and a relationship that will be with them forever. I wish my grandchildren could have a similar experience. Unfortunately, I don't have the financial resources Puny had. Francesca was Allegra's patient victim. She alternated being the client when Allegra wanted to be a hairdresser, or her maid and gofer when Allegra needed something.

On her lucky days, she was Alberto's bride, if Allegra decided to be a wedding coordinator.

Giacomo was less willing to be bossed around, but the two of them were required to pay a toll for coming into the lower level of the villa where we lived. Regardless of all the abuses, Francesca and Giacomo grew up as close to our children as logistics permitted, and I'm happy for it.

In August we were going to Crans sur Sierre in Switzerland, where we had purchased an apartment, and where we spent occasional vacations from Christmas or February school break. I think we all had great times. We had a lot of friends and some relatives there, including Allegra's nemesis, Maddalena. I never saw hate at first sight, like that. Maddalena is the daughter of Manuel, the cousin who moved to Bronxville with us. He has an apartment in Montana, near Crans. The summer before the move to the States, we got together, so that our children could get to know each other. The look that the two girls exchanged when they met for the first time was one of pure disdain, and it has never gotten better.

In spite of that, I have fond memories of Crans, including Paolo's greatest fishing achievement. Paolo was probably eight years old, and decided to enter an adult fishing tournament on the occasion of local village feast. The competitors were all adult, and expert fishermen, at least if we judged them by their fishing gear. Beginner's luck or talent - Paolo won First Prize for the largest fish caught, and also First Prize for the most fish caught. He should also have won the prize for the fisherman who came from the greatest distance. The local jury. however, was quite annoyed that a little kid was cleaning up all the honors, and gave that prize to someone who came from Germany.

In Bronxville, in the meantime, we were making new friends: some Italian and some local. Our closest Italian friends were the Carellas, a family from Genoa that we had not known before. Clelia, the mother, was a friend of my sister Bernardetta's, and Gian, her husband, knew many of my friends from Giovanni's soccer team. Their oldest son, Cristiano, was in Paolo's grade, and was part of his closest group of friends. I owe a lot to the Carellas, they fed me and kept me company during the summers while my family was away, and Gian gave badly needed business to my newly formed company. He volunteered that without waiting for me to ask for his help.

Our best American friends were the Taylors. They moved to Bronxville from Chicago one year after we arrived. Kate became Silvia's best friend despite the fact that they had two very different personalities. Terry and I – though we grew up continents apart - were amazed by the similarity of our record collections, our shared interest in sports, (soccer in particular), and the movie genre we both liked.

On the business side, things were not going well for Costa. The company was over- leveraged because of expanding too much in every division. At the time, the interest payments due the banks were as high as 15%. The profits of the business could not cover that. There was a real possibility of bankruptcy. Furthermore, the legal structure of Costa was such, that all the shareholders – meaning all the cousins - were personally responsible for the company's debts. (A similar situation to that of Lloyds of London Insurance Company). Consultants were brought in, and it was strongly suggested that we divest, and concentrate our resources in the business that had the most potential: the cruise line. The consultants also suggested that we make the company more attractive to outside investor by cutting back on the family members in management, and bringing in outside managers.

That was a bitter pill to swallow for most of us. The company and family culture of equal partnership, and hard work for the common good, had guided us for four generation, but could no longer continue. In addition, the sacrifices were not evenly distributed, because the family members in the oil, textile, and cargo divisions saw their jobs go on the block, while some of the cousins in the passenger division were allowed to keep working. An infusion of new capital was also necessary, and all of us sold real estate, or forfeited money that we had loaned to the company. The much loved villas in Rapallo had to be sacrificed, and places that had been part of our upbringing were gone.

My sisters had loaned money that they had inherited from our parents to the company, and now there was an attempt to have them forfeit their credit as well. It was clearly an injustice, because as women, they had not enjoyed the past good fortunes of the company, and it was only fair that they be left out of the current misfortune. Eventually, they received real estate instead of cash, and while the evaluations of what they received was probably above the real value at the time, in the long run it was more advantageous for them. It was amazing that we remained united, even though the sacrifices were not equal.

It was decided to consolidate the three main offices in the USA: Chicago, New York and Miami; a measure I had suggested before, but which had not been accepted by Genoa. The head office would be in Miami. I was hoping to be selected for that position, but Emanuele out-maneuvered me, and was chosen. I was offered the responsibility for the new holding company that was based in Holland. That position required our family to return to Italy, and for me, it meant frequent trips to Amsterdam. Silvia and I had to make the decision of going back or remaining in the States. It was not as agonizing as it might sound. The option of returning to a safe job in Torino with zio Piero, was quickly eliminated because of total opposition by Silvia.

Returning, and accepting Costa's offer, would have meant relocating, and for the children, adjusting to new schools and classmates. We did not want to impose that sacrifice upon them. In addition, we judged that Italy would offer fewer opportunities for them in the future. So we decided to stay in the USA.

16

Royal Costa

The next question was what should I do about a job? So far, I had only worked for the family company, and I had a hard time picturing myself working in a subordinate position. Furthermore, I was a foreigner, without the network of friends and relatives useful when looking for a job. I decided to go into business for myself. I had recommended to Genoa that one way to improve the company was to create a tour department with travel packages that would include cruises, and other aspects of a vacation. The industry was evolving from traditional shipping into tourism. Offering complete vacations rather than just cruises would create new possibilities. My proposal never took off. It was impossible to start a new division while trying to cope with the problems resulting from over-expansion. I offered to do it on my own, if the company would use me as a supplier. The problem was that my experience as tour operator was minimal, and without capital to back me, I had no room for error. Our lawyer, Stephen Galef, had a friend in the travel business. Until recently, Sedat Palti had been the operator of Pan Am Airlines in Italy, and had lost the business when Pan Am decided to run it in house. Like me, he was unsure if he should stay in Rome or move to the States. When we got together, our plan was that he would supply clients and operational know-how, and I would supply the Costa business and managerial experience. Things did not work out that way. He only had two or three clients, and the business from Costa was up in the air, lost in the complexities of reorganization.

We did not know all that on February, 1982, when we incorporated Royal Costa Tours. Besides the two of us, the company consisted of my secretary, Luigia, who had great confidence in my ability to create a profitable company quickly. The office was located in an area of the old Costa's office under construction to accommodate a new tenant. For quite some time, we worked in the dust with electric wires hanging over us, and walls yet to be erected. Sedi is a unique person. Extremely superstitious, with wide swings of mood - either on top of the world, or in the deepest hole. He did not help at that time because he was more interested in putting together a garbage disposal deal than soliciting his old clients. My friend, Gian Carella, saved our young company by giving us all his company's travel business, which was worth about half a million dollars. He did that without me even asking for it. He just felt I needed help and came forward. That, plus a few other operations, allowed us to get through our first year; after that, more business came in. We developed a nice client base, and in 1986, we had many groups booked for European traffic. In April of that year, however, President Reagan decided to bomb Libya because of their terrorist activities. In one week we saw more than one million dollars worth of business evaporate. Clients afraid of the political situation cancelled their plans, and we were again in hot water.

I was quite discouraged to see three years of work ruined by an unforeseen event. Mom was the one who helped me keep things in perspective, insisting that I had not wasted my time in dead end work. She decided to start working herself, having more free time with the children in school full time. The Benetton Company was very popular in New York, and were opening new stores for children. It took us a while, but we convinced the local representative to give us an agreement to open a store, and we opened on the corner of Lexington Avenue and 72nd street. Mom worked there every day until three PM, when she returned home to help with the homework. For the first couple of years the sales were very good. Eventually, Benetton opened too many stores; the Gap copied its product line at much lower prices, and the brand lost its edge. After five years we decided to close the store. Nevertheless, it was a good experience. We did not make much money on the venture, but in 1986 I needed to be busy with something other than tourism, and must of all, Mom realized that she could be a good mother and work at the same time. She was a very anxious mother, afraid that the children would be exposed to risks and situations that you were not prepared to handle. It was hard for her to let the kids go, and allow them to live their own lives. The Benetton work experience enriched her life, and helped her to accept the fact that the children were going to be their own people, and function without her protection.

In the meantime, the drastic medicine administered to Costa began to have results. The company was able to start a badly needed program of new ships constructions. First the Riviera, then the Marina, and then the Allegra (named after our Allegra) joined the fleet. These three vessels were totally reconstructed from old hulls. The Classica and the Romantica – they arrived few years later – were completely new constructions. By the mid-nineties, under the guidance of my cousin Nicola, the company became the leader in the European and South American cruise market, and a worthy competitor in the Caribbean. By then, the company was publicly traded on the Italian stock exchange. At the beginning, the family held majority control of the stock. We then sold twenty percent of our shares to the French company, Accord, with a sindacate agreement to retain control. The first phase of the restructuring was completed, and it was a painful, stressful process. It was amazing that we, the partners, stuck together with remarkable harmony through it. I think the education and discipline we received from our fathers, and the leisure time we spent together in Rapallo had something to do with it.

At this point the family had different interests. The few members still working for the company were keen to hold on to control, and to expand the business. The majority of the others were interested in receiving dividends or cash for their shares. To the credit of those still working for the company, they followed the will of the majority, and we began to look for possible buyers.

We controlled a large market share in the European cruise business, and that was very appealing to such companies as Royal Caribbean and Carnival. At that time, they operated mostly in the Caribbean, and were looking for new markets. We negotiated with both companies, and at the end of March, 1997, a contract was signed with Carnival.

The price we obtained was in line with our most optimistic projection. It is ironic, however, that Royal Caribbean which had the losing bid, eventually ended up buying a similar company for a much higher price. In Genoa, there is a fitting adage, " Sell, take your profit and regret". In retrospect, it is sad to have witnessed the end of the work of four generations, and to see our company's culture disappear. We were, however, like dinosaurs in a fast changing world, and our last hurrah was to have saved the company from extinction.

Back at Royal Costa, we managed to survive the Libyan crisis with the help of a large number of clients from Costa Italy, who went to the Caribbean for winter cruises. For a few years the situation was difficult, but manageable. We had a big breakthrough a few years later, when the new president of Costa Miami decided to promote Mediterranean cruises. He wanted to know what could be done to create a more complete European experience for clients, and how to promote it. At that time, the last flight from Europe to the USA left around two PM, and the arrival time of the ships did not coincide with that, which meant that passengers could not catch that flight on the same day. We suggested that as Costa was already paying for one night's free stay in Europe for those passengers who had bought air transportation in addition to the cruise, Costa might as well pay for a second night, and promote "Two Nights - Stay Free in Europe when you cruise with Costa!". The additional cost for the promotion was minimal. The offer was a huge success, and was repeated for many years to come. We had so many requests, that hotel space in cities like Venice, Rome and Amsterdam became a problem. Here is where Sedi came through with his experience and connections, and we were always able to solve these operational problems. Success bred success, and the clients who were not buying air transportation from Costa came to us to buy services in Europe. A second cruise line, Royal Olympic, became a client, and business was good. We moved to larger offices, and had fifteen full time employees in Rome, Miami, and New York, plus seasonal help. In Genoa, we started a joint partnership with my brother Giovanni, using his offices and one of his employees.

17

An Ending…And A Beginning

Mom, after the Benetton experience, decided that she needed something to which she could dedicate herself, now that the children needed less of her presence It was hard for her to accept, but she was realistic enough to know it was the right thing. She experimented: working in retail in Bronxville, doing volunteer work with terminal cancer patients, and also with sick children. This last suited her personality, and she wanted to do it in a more professional way. She attended a course at Sarah Lawrence College for Women that wanted to reenter the work force. In her youth she had never been a good student, and she had doubts that she could keep up with the curriculum, there was also the difficulty of the different language. She proved herself wrong, passed all the exams brilliantly, and graduated. She was very proud of herself, and enjoyed my admiration. Her degree allowed her to enroll in a two-year course to become a patient advocate. A patient advocate was a relatively new position in hospitals. Advocates helped patients make sure that all their rights were protected, and that they received proper counseling. She was very excited at the idea of helping people in need. In the meantime, it was our Silver Wedding Anniversary, and as much as I hate surprise parties the one the children organized for us was a pleasant, unexpected event. Life again was very good, just as it had been in 1956, and I should have been on the alert. Well, I was taken by surprise again. Now don't get me wrong, I'm not implying that it's wrong to enjoy your good moments. What I mean is that you should always be aware of reality, remembering that we are not invincible, or above life's hurdles.

Mom went to Crans in August to spend some time with Puny, and she started to experience strong headaches especially in the morning. She went to see our doctor when she got back to Bronxville, and he diagnosed it as stress, probably due to the exams she had studied for. He prescribed an MRI

- just in case. We went to White Plains Hospital on a Saturday in September, and on Sunday I left for Europe, on a pre-planned business trip.

My first stop actually was not business. I went to Lanzo to visit with Puny, Piero and Camilla. We were having dinner on Monday night when we received a frightened call from Mom. Our doctor had phoned that he wanted to see her because the MRI showed some abnormality. I flew back the next morning and you all remember the tragedy that followed. All I can say is that I'm proud of all of you - the way you lived through those difficult months. We were a family, and we cared for each other in spite of the unavoidable tensions we all felt. It was as hard for Allegra to leave college and care for Mom, as it was for Paolo to stay away in school and not spend time with her. It was admirable for Al to go through his senior year, football practice and college decisions and not be discouraged, or give up. For her part, Mom – who before had always been afraid of illness - was showing great courage, and never panicked or complained. She taught us a lesson in love, dignity and perseverance. She never indulged in self-pity and always showed her sense of humor. We all became better people because of the years we spent with her, but in her last months, she really showed us what type of integrity we needed to have. That made her loss even harder to take.

We were all sad, wounded, and afraid of what was coming next in our lives. I think we all learned from Mom's legacy, and continued to live as she would have us do: in the present. I said something similar at Paolo and Wendy's rehearsal dinner. but I guess repeating myself is a prerogative of the old people. You cannot live in the past. The past gives us experience, and the memory of the loved ones we lost, and we always need to remember, but if we can't go forward our lives are finished. You cannot live in the future. It is good to have dreams, and make plans, but to turn them into reality you need to act today. So I wish you to be able to appreciate what every day brings you. If you think nothing is going on, and you are living a boring routine, it means you need to notice all the beautiful things constantly happening around you, and become enthusiastic about them. Take the long view, and don't be discouraged or over enthusiastic by what happen today. Eventually, what is logical, decent, and just, will prevail. Don't be afraid of what is new, or ashamed to be out of fashion.

To be progressive or conservative is just a label, and neither are absolutely right. Rejecting something, just because it's unfamiliar, is wrong. It is also wrong to embrace new ideas without questioning their validity. Always use your brain, and do your homework, and don't accept at face value what you have been told. Always ask questions, don't be too lazy or disinterested to know. Be a pain in the neck, but don't be afraid to express your opinion if you think it is important; just be mindful of the feelings of others. Sometime it's wiser to eat crow than say something you might regret later on. After everything is said though, the most important thing is your family. Love each other, and be superior to all petty reasons for disunity.

And now you have it, I gave you my lecture. As I said, don't take it at face value, judge with your brain and your heart. One thing is sure, however, if you care for each other you'll be okay.